Michelle Hoffman lives and leads with hope and grit despite the way-too-soon experience of losing her beloved Sean. We've had the honor of watching Michelle take this book from brainstorm to birth and know that many will benefit from her warmth, hard-won wisdom, and practical advice.

–Guy Kawasaki, Best Selling Author
–Beth Kawasaki, Marketing Strategy Consultant

Reading *Life Worth Living* is like having a dear friend who really cares about you sitting at your dining room table, reassuring you warmly, and sometimes making you laugh. I am not a widow, but I learned much from this book. I learned that people can rebuild a joyful life when they must, and surprisingly, that there's a hero within us when we have to navigate a new, complex world. Michelle gets it. She knows people and can teach us something about being human in both good and not-so-good times.

–Julie Won, Partner at Hanson & Doremus Investment Management

I just met with a dear friend for coffee. Her husband died three months ago. She has found great comfort and wisdom in Michelle Hoffmann's book as she goes through her grief. She plans on reaching out to Michelle at some point, but until she's ready, it made my heart happy to know that my friend has been helped through Michelle's wisdom.

Thank you for writing your book, Michelle. I've looked into the eyes of someone who has been touched by your story.

–Lesley Moffat, Author & Certified Life Coach at mPowered Educator

What does it really mean to move forward through grieving This spectacular debut novel from life coach Michelle Hoffmann deals with a difficult subject -- grieving the loss of a loved partner -- in an exceptional way. *Life Worth Living* focuses on the steps to recovering the joy of living, in a brave and touching story, filled with the humor, compassion, and practical skills that Ms. Hoffmann brings. While the book was written for widows raising children, there is something here for everyone. As we all face the loss of those we cherish, and reach for meaning in the process of living with and embracing our memories while moving forward toward the lightness of joy in our lives.

–Leslee L. Martin, Market Risk Coordinator - Federal Reserve Bank of San Francisco

For anyone who has survived the loss of a loved one, this book is like finding a trail of breadcrumbs that will lead you back to the light. Poignant. Raw. Real. Beautiful. Michelle gently guides her readers through the heavy fog of grief, reminding them that life can heal and begin again.

–Erin Kelley-Smith, Featured Author & Life Coach

This is a subject that so many find so difficult to articulate and understand. Finally a book that is part friend and part guide during a journey that no-one wishes or imagines. Michelle's authenticity and vulnerability will guide the widow, widower, family, friend or coworker to a life worth living.

–Meredith Peterson, Real Estate Specialist

You made me laugh …and cry…which I guess is a good thing.

–J Djurovic, Parent

Life Worth Living is the most helpful book on loss I never wanted to read. Loss is so crippling and heavy, and feels like it will never end but this author shows it can be done. Thank you for writing this Michelle Hoffmann. It's good to know that that even after loss there is a life worth living.

–Debra Pearson, Bestselling Author

One of my favorite parts in the book: So, what do you do? You sit down and figure out what you need in your life. And you make sure you don't waste your life energy on things that don't make a positive difference. I haven't really sat down to plan anything. I may need a guide for this...

–T Nguyn, Parent

Life Worth Living is soooo authentic, real, YOU. It is put together in a great order. You touched my heart with your last dance with Sean and memories of your first dance. "I see you. I hear you & what you say matters." It is so good.

–Christina Voissom, Bereavement Coordinator and Counselor

Michelle has beautifully captured, with raw honesty, her innermost feelings and coping strategies to help others overcome the heartbreak of losing a partner and aid resilience for themselves and their children. *Life Worth Living* is a must read for those looking for practical and caring advice to help overcome the hardest event a person will ever have to face.

–Rosie Foster, National Manager- Health and
Personal Injury at Perpetual Limited, Australia

How do we navigate through our grief so that we can take care of ourselves and our children? Michelle has sailed these waters. Her heartfelt anecdotes and advice help readers see that while the journey may not be smooth, we are not alone. She provides a map to lead us out of the storm.

–**Karyn Watanabe**, English Teacher, Liberty High School

Life Worth Living is a girlfriend's' guide to managing widowhood, I'm not a widow and have not been through a devastating loss. BUT, I would feel good handing anyone I care about this book so someone with this expertise, like Michelle Hoffmann, can help guide them through the process.

–**Victoria Lavi**, Marketing Consultant

More than a road map through the grieving journey, Michelle Hoffmann provides practical and inspiring ideas for living a whole and positively healthy life.

–**Cynthia Rekar**, Business and Consumer Insights/Market Research Professional

Part of the joy of *Life Worth Living* is relating to Michelle despite the sad topic.

I kept reading as if Michelle were talking to me, then would stop and think I'm not a widow, this isn't for me, until I realized it is for me because I can adopt this advice to my current situation in life. Michelle's expert words help all people find a true vision and achieve basic goals of love, health and financial freedom. Michelle Hoffmann is my inspiration!

–**Kira Edwards**, Real Estate Investor

Life Worth Living is a heartfelt and inspirational guide to dealing with grief, helping your children through their loss and moving on with your life in a meaningful and fulfilling way. Hoffmann shares her own insights and experiences, laying out concrete steps for both emotional and practical issues a new widow has to deal with. But, more than that, Hoffmann manages to share her unique energy and spark of life in a way that will help anyone reading this book look at their life choices differently, strive to be the best version of themselves, and truly live a life worth living. I felt like she was right next to me, cheering me on as I read each page.

–Ann Pianin DeHovitz, School administrator

Life Worth Living is a beautifully written book. It follows the heart-wrenching experience of a widow who needs to provide for grieving children and deal with numerous practical challenges while coping with her own grief. Although it is hard to keep your eyes dry while reading it, the book is ultimately uplifting and empowering, leaving the reader feeling like they've just spent hours sharing heartbreak and getting advice and support from their closest and most supportive friend.

–Susan Athey, Professor at Stanford Graduate School of Business

Your hindsight gives me great foresight! Without your guidance I would be years behind my current state. Thank you for your experience and expertise in walking the widow(er)'s journey. Your best practices help me answer my own questions in life.

–Aaron Howard, Wealth Advisor, Widower

Life Worth Living

LIFE WORTH LIVING

*A Practical and Compassionate
Guide to Navigating Widowhood
and Sole Parenting*

MICHELLE HOFFMANN

NEW YORK

LONDON • NASHVILLE • MELBOURNE • VANCOUVER

Life Worth Living

A Practical and Compassionate Guide to Navigating Widowhood and Sole Parenting

Published in New York, New York, by Morgan James Publishing in partnership with Difference Press. Morgan James is a trademark of Morgan James, LLC. www.MorganJamesPublishing.com

ISBN 9781642796650 paperback
ISBN 9781642796667 eBook
ISBN 9781642796674 audio
Library of Congress Control Number: 2019943035

Cover Design Concept: Leslie Messmer & Jennifer Stimson

Cover Design & Interior Design: Chris Treccani   www.3dogcreative.net

Editor: Moriah Howell

Book Coaching: The Author Incubator

Morgan James is a proud partner of Habitat for Humanity Peninsula and Greater Williamsburg. Partners in building since 2006.

Get involved today! Visit
MorganJamesPublishing.com/giving-back

I dedicate this book to my late husband, Sean, who, although now in my past, showed me the value of true love. To our children, Kevin and Rachel, who, besides giving me a reason to live in the present and enjoy a Life Worth Living, show they will innovate a positive legacy for the future.

TABLE OF CONTENTS

ON BECOMING A WIDOW

On becoming a widow, I cannot share the joys you would have absolutely loved.

On becoming a widow, I have had to make all the decisions I chose to share or previously bounce off you, my beloved.

On becoming a widow, I have felt an empty space where you once walked, held my hand and kept me company in a crowd.

On becoming a widow, I have become a holding place for others who loved you to be close to you. But I am not you and they are disappointed in me for not seeing you when they look to me.

On becoming a widow, there are those who used to bring us joy who now avoid me because without you I am not who they are looking for and it is too painful for them to be with just my half of us.

At your funeral, I was so authentically overjoyed to see friends and loved ones, community members and leaders, people we have shared time with because of distance and other everyday responsibilities. They left their lives for a moment to be with me and the children as we honor you and your life. You would have loved to see them, every one. I wished to spend five days with each of them. My joy was effervescent until something reminded me that you were by my side in only an ethereal way.

At your funeral, my joy of the attendees buoyed me as I realized a few things. One, the reason we were there, and two, going through with the reason we were there. It had not been long since I had been without you. Now it has.

Has the pain of making the right decision to let you go dulled over time? Not really. It was still the right choice. It wasn't a choice. It was my deepest, loving, compassionate decision to say, "It's okay to go." You didn't want to go. I didn't want you to go. That doesn't stop making it a hard decision to say it was okay. I make all the decisions now.

Decisions on what is best in the long run. Decisions on what is right for our family right now, decisions on where to sleep and what to eat and how to act and … and the decision that rolling in a fetal position and mourning your loss does not benefit anyone if that is the only decision.

I've made the decision to live on, to walk our path, and live out our decisions without you by my side.

Living is a decision. How to live is a multi-faceted series of other decisions. Deciding to live is only the first step. Then there is a cascade of choices on how to live. Some think it is not a choice. I choose to believe I have made the choice and I can at least influence my decisions.

Then there are the decisions to follow other's guidance or choose for myself. I sifted through those who felt it is their judgmental prerogative and responsibility to make decisions for me because you are not there to collaborate in making them. I'm not incapable of making them. I just don't think that what is right for others is always right for the children and me. That decision took a little while to figure out because I know their help is well-intended. Then I had to decide to thank them and do it my way.

My first decision was to not make some decisions until I was ready to make them. After making 14,327 decisions I never wanted to make, I could start to make decisions that would move us forward.

Which way do I continue our journey now? Knowing that doing nothing was not an option, I had to choose. But what should I choose? So, I elected what you and I chose together to start my confidence building my mantra: "I can do this."

Some things I had to decide not to decide until another time. I compartmentalized the decision-making. That way, I only had to decide on a percent of the changes that needed to be made at a time.

You and I made choices together and I can honor you and rebuild myself by moving forward with our positive choices. Others may not understand, they were never part of the decision-making process, so it is not expected of them.

I miss you. I wasn't done with you yet. We weren't through. We didn't make nearly enough decisions together. When I am uncertain, I go to the quiet place in my mind and ask for your guidance. You hold me and reassure me I should navigate forward and guide others along the journey. I continue to be a widow and I continue to make all the decisions.

My new companion, grief, accompanies me as I make every attempt to remain in balance addressing each aspect of life for me and the children. I have accepted our situation. I know you didn't wish to leave. You gave me all you had, down to your last breath, which you used to tell me you loved me.

I've forgiven anyone whose efforts were not quite well-intended. I acknowledge the people I rely on for emotional and inspirational support. I am grateful to those who share their subject matter expertise, networking, and accountability to ensure I remain on my newly-developed track. I negotiate legal and financial paperwork to ensure we preserve assets and update my intentions. I do everything in my power to remain healthy and select lifestyle choices that remind us life is worth living, so we thrive rather than just wait out our days. I center all of my decisions on the children, because they are the center of everything. The children are my reason for waking up and getting enough sleep at night. I make every decision to stabilize, support and help the children grow in the right trajectory for them. So, they too can say they lived a full and happy life ... even though you are not here to walk with us any longer.

When I think about deciding to be vulnerable enough again to find someone new to trust in our decision-making, I wonder what would make someone want to decide with me? I know I can love as deeply as we loved each other. It is not the same world you left. We'll see if I can decide to do that again. That is not a decision I need to make today.

On Becoming a Widow's Guide

Since becoming a widow, I have solitarily made a multitude of significant decisions. I've changed my identity, role, and career. I've even adjusted the Circle of Trust on my Relationship Spiral, (which I will explain) building my own Advisory Board to tap into when I need them. It was difficult to realize I could find new ways to have fun, even without you. I have found diversion and entertainment, laughter and joy again. I attempt to respect myself and the need for "down-time" to refuel so I can be fully present with the children and in my work.

The children and I are so deeply grateful and I try to express my gratitude to our family, friends, community, related by blood, related by love and those unrelated for sharing their skills, expertise, resources, network, energy, love, affection, and acceptance with us all along the way. We are buoyed by all their support.

I believe being a widow and sole parent is a specific set of circumstances and there has not been a guide for it, until now. I am called upon to act as a guide through this profoundly life-altering experience because I intimately understand the tragedy of the loss of a loved one. I write this for others who cannot see their future and want to put their life back together and feel compelled to live again... happy, without spending years suffering in grief, crying, fearful they aren't really living their lives or being the parent, their children need. I help widows who are ready to continue on with life as a widow and sole parent and want to create and live a full and happy life after loss. Widowhood is a huge life-role change. Navigating widowhood and sole parenting is vital; don't orphan the children. We find teachers and mentors when we need to learn something important. So, I compiled a practical and compassionate guide to remind them that even when they're responsible for taking care of everyone and everything, I can show them how they can still have dreams of their own. Widows and their children are valuable and have a life worth living...and I will hold their hand and walk this journey with them.

CHAPTER 1:

She Was Only Planning Dinner

Hello Gorgeous,

If I could undo this for you, I would. (I can only imagine that is what my circle of loved ones felt for me when my husband died.)

I met Jennifer once as the leader of the Girl Scout Leaders … and I was a Girl Scout Leader. Her husband, a high school friend of mine, and I went running occasionally to prepare for my first half-marathon. When I learned he had gone for a run, had a heart attack, and died, I must have felt like everyone else who was shocked and saddened and didn't know what to do.

But I *knew* what to do because I had gone through it. In fact, I knew I couldn't do nothing, because unfortunately, I had lost my husband and intimately know the tragedy of the loss of a loved one. She was only planning dinner and suddenly she faced planning a wedding-sized community extravaganza memorial. Despite her incredible project management and planning skills, she was grieving the loss of her husband and remaining a steadfast pillar of strength for her children. She joined a club she was never intending to join; the initiation is too dear: the widow's club. I couldn't fix it for her. I could bring food to her home, give her a hug and say, "This will never be okay. I will hold your hand and walk this journey with you. I am close enough you can trust me and not so close that you need to worry about my emotions. Let's project manage this thing." Jennifer introduced me to the mourners in the living room who exhaled a sigh of relief that someone could take the lead.

How do you continue on with your life as a widow and sole parent? That is your journey now. I write this book to you and anyone who must walk this path after losing their partner and co-parent. You have made the choice to walk the path you and your late husband planned, without him. It will be different as you step into your new future. Now it is time to recreate your plans.

I will walk this journey with you and guide you on what I call "the rebuild" as you use the tools in this book to gain control in an out-of-control situation to identify, manifest, and navigate your course to a full and happy life as a widow and sole-parent. You have become the head of the household, a role you previously shared with your partner. Your priorities have changed and all the decisions are up to you to make.

It feels overwhelming. Who should you trust and who is trying to up-sell you, to a more expensive phone plan? You are creating your Inspirational Advisory Board ensuring you are not vulnerable. You are re-establishing your future by taking over more than just the role your late husband filled, besides becoming a Subject Matter Expert filling in any gaps of knowledge you previously relied on him for. That, combined with supporting grieving children, often leaves little room to take care of yourself. All the while putting surrogate role models in place to support your grieving children in the four areas where children are most vulnerable: peer groups, family unit, school, and community, including the transition time so you don't have to be the only one driving six hours a day to and from their extracurricular activities to maintain their success trajectories. You set aside one-on-one time with each of them so they no longer feel jealousy that you are spending more attention on one, while what you would prefer doing is curl up in bed wishing things would just fall into place, including dinner on the table.

That is a lot. In Jennifer's case, I am honored to have the privilege of being her widow/sole-parent guide. As she focuses on health and self-care, I get to be her personal fitness trainer to prepare for a 5K run, which is extra terrifying for her because her husband died while out on a run. (That reminded her to work her life backward by ensuring things like her will and updated life insurance are in place.) I walked her through an insightful exercise as I evaluated and guided her posture as she was walking/running. I invited her to make observations as she was walking forward with her head tipped down to look at her feet. She said that her windpipe felt closed down so it was hard to breathe, her peripheral vision narrowed, and she could only see her immediate present. Tipping her head up high created another closed airway and an equally difficult peripheral vision situation. It was difficult-to-impossible for her to tip her head up to the point she could not see where she was in the present moment or where her feet were taking her. Knocked off balance, she was challenged to see far ahead literally and metaphorically into the future. Adjusting her view to just slightly above horizon allowed an open airway for easy breathing, full peripheral vision, and the opportunity to not only see where she is in the present, but where she is intending to go. It is a physical exercise that provided her with insight into how she was feeling in the moment. She is stabilizing herself and her children in the present with targets into the future. She is now looking ahead far enough to breathe easily and see her future clearly.

Like Jennifer, you are assessing your situation and accepting where you are at, setting your targets and deciding to move into the direction of who you would like to become and how you can best guide your children. Not everyone has a perfect partner. Regardless, you are now in the position to handle everything. It's overwhelming to get through life's celebrations without your late husband, create new traditions, honor old ones that come with grief and gratitude. The path you set with your loved one differs from your life now. You are still alive. What you are doing is good enough. It's actually super fantastic! You can find control in a situation wherein you may feel out of control. You are expecting a lot of yourself. So, let me remind you: you are safe, loved, and not alone. Keep moving forward.

There are three steps to moving through grief:

1. A desire to move through grief
2. Acknowledge what grief represents to you
3. Determine how holding that grief will serve you going forward in your life

Step four of the three steps is to assess whether you are ready to face step one. How do you know if you are ready? Sometimes hunkering down and holding on, pulling in your energy and resources is the right thing to do to prepare for growth. If you are not ready to address step one it will feel like a cliff. When you are ready, you will beg for the next phase.

Grief is complicated and ambiguous. Even as you learn to live without the physical presence of your missing person it is impossible to find complete closure. However, finding meaning in the relationship's value and touchstones to connect in your heart and honoring your loved one in physical ways is helpful to distance and reduce the aftershocks and discover your perception of what the loss means to you. This poem is how grief and I have addressed our relationship to the point of camaraderie over the loss of my husband. I went from, what I call, functionally catatonic to setting life priorities which brought me to hold the hand and walk the widow's journey with Jennifer, and now others.

Grief and Gratitude by Michelle Hoffmann

Grief owns you

Grief is like a boa constrictor gently wrapping itself around you

Slowly stroking and lulling you into a paralyzed hypnosis

Absorbing your thoughts with mesmerizing focus

Curling, curdling, caressing, until it envelopes your existence into its full heat

Encroaching on your life, demanding your attention, owning your thoughts, violating your dreams, dismissing your hopes

Grief grins, opens itself to you and sucks you in, embracing you wholly.

Grief blinds you from seeing anything not in its grasp. It forces your face away from the future

Allowing only the past to cross your path, over and over, again and again, polishing the memories in hopes they do not pass and pass away.

You may grasp and grapple to escape grief but its hold is secure and leaves you restricted, breathless

Grief grins, knowing you'll never fulfill your deepest wishes and desires.

Grief is the event horizon on a black hole sucking you into the gap where your love once held you strong. And you make the choice not to be sucked into the vacuum that threatens your life and existence.

Grief is not to blame. Grief is not the culprit. It's what grief holds that holds you down, fetal,

Wound tightly in a cocoon oppressed by its force and insistence. You transform against your will.

You did not invite grief into your party, your life your family or home.

Grief is an unwelcome dinner guest ruining your appetite, your party dress, blocking out joy,

Mocking laughter, unveiling unhelpful advice

Anguish clouding the air and usurping the oxygen in the room

Demanding the conversation

Buzzkill, outperforming, all-consuming enveloping, suffocating, flooring, gasping, grasping

Grief is a demanding companion, insisting on hoarding your time, thoughts conversation, consideration

Stopping you in your tracks, weighing you down paralyzing thoughts and movement

Grief roams the house at night, smothering the children to sleep.

Grief is insistent on stealing you from what you are trying to get accomplished, grabbing you from any moment of faith forward and slamming your head against the wall, dropping you to the kitchen floor, with its foot on your neck, waiting you out, time healing all wounds, gurgling in your own puddle of despair for who is no longer there.

Grief holds you, embracing you close, whispering in your ear. Grief clenches your heart, compressing your ribs.

In the name of love, grief stifles your screams for release or an attempt to catch your breath. Grief grabs you … holds you down while you reel and squirm, struggling for escape for air, light a glimmer of future release, a sound of….

While grief grins knowing it can outlast your vulnerability in its all-encompassing grasp.

And when grief has cracked your ribs, misshapen your life and limbs and wiped your hope of future, pulled you into its realm

You then realize there is strength in the vulnerability.

It is up to you to snatch a snip of air, succumb to the monster knowing it will never leave you … nor do you wish it to go

Because grief shelters the greatest love you've ever known

Just out of grasp, grief holds the light and joy of love so great its loss could inflict enduring pain of equal depth.

And you hold on to grief in fear that releasing it or even if it loosens its hold, you might lose the memory of love so intense its loss is too great a burden to bear … much too much of a loss … a loss greater than grief's company.

So you and grief confront one another, unwelcome bedfellows, back-seat driver, green with envy at the sight of others' joy of what could have been….

Grief grins as you push it off your lap and out of your hair allowing it space at the table in the empty chair.

You talk to grief wary of it as a threat

Pleading it to move on but not willing to let it go

You ask advice of grief and wish it would hold you close without holding you down or holding you back

Grief is company but grief doesn't give support or strength.

Grief requests acknowledgment and honor in exchange for freedom and respect.

And the love grief holds, holds you gently, gently loosening the grip of grief

Until you tame grief into a space that allows in a breath, a thought, a sanctuary, where you and love lost meet to share memories.

And after tears and a cup of tea, grief grins and steps back for a while allowing you to make your bed and look in the mirror to see what's left of the scorched landscape and where to go from here, with grief walking alongside, honored. Honored to have been present and part of your life. Forever changed.

When you are ready which is not nearly soon enough, grief grins and releases lost love to walk alongside you, reminding you of your value in a whispering wind across your ear. Grief shows up long enough to remind you to feel the range of emotions to live life fully with grief being the far end of the number line.

Grief grins, reminding you to feel the depth of joy as fully as you felt the depth of grief, because one does not exist without the other.

And you hold grief in a safe place, grateful for having had the depth of love as deep as the depth of the pain of loss showing that you are living fully.

Confidence Assessment

When you are ready to honor what grief holds for you, the next phase is to assess where you are at in different aspects of your life. You can add categories to your assessment. To start, here are questions to ask yourself:

T/F I'm 100 percent sure I have clear goals and know exactly the steps to take to achieve a worthy future for myself and success for my children.

T/F I'm 100 percent sure I have secured all the financial and legal requirements to close my husband's "estate" and I've updated all my end-of-life documents and plans.

T/F I'm 100 percent sure I've got the resources and the right people in place to help propel me toward my goals and dreams and support the children's success in theirs.

T/F I'm 100 percent sure of my health and I'm a role model for my children in my self-care regime. I have a healthy regime established for myself and my children.

T/F I'm 100 percent sure the children are moving through grief and loss and have support systems in place to guide them on successful trajectories unique to them.

T/F I'm 100 percent sure I am surrounded by the right people and activities and can help others move through the grief and loss of my husband.

T/F I'm 100 percent sure I find time to have fun and diversion doing things I love that replenish my energy so I can enjoy a life worth living.

If you are not at 100 percent, what percentage would you give to your confidence level right now?

CHAPTER 2:

Shattered

Shattered by Michelle Hoffmann

Shattered, shattered, shattered, shattered
The glass tears at my feet
a burning reminder of the fragility of life
Life in the balance,
Balancing durability
And breakability
Resisting the pressure
To persist despite its frailty
Sturdy enough to endure
Delicate enough to shatter
Shattered.
Noise scaring evil spirits
Evil spirits daring to mar our joyous celebration
Waking me
Confirming a contract

A contract to walk on glass for you
Treating you with special care, special, as you treat me
Shatter, Sh, Sh, Sh, at, her
Hushing me to sweep up so others are not hurt
Feelings are not hurt
No reminders of the loss of what once was
What will never be the same
I cannot, after all, put shattered glass back together
As this glass shatters, so may you never break
Reminders of sadness and sorrow
You pull joyful memories from a black bag
To bring us back to the moment
And forward together
Our life together as difficult to break
As it would be to piece together the broken glass
Like glass, life is so fragile
So fragile that we should enjoy each moment
As if it were our last together
Shattered, leaving me in shards
Of our first and last kiss
Of everything in between
Light redirected and refracted
Sparks in every direction
Leaving me
With the responsibility
Leaving me
Shattered.

My Whole World Has Changed

"My whole world has just changed," is what I said when I first met Sean. We fell in love instantly. Well, that is not true, it took a few hours. If you don't know the story, my cousin and I were on a cruise at the wrong dinner seating at the wrong dinner table, seated with these two guys. One guy she couldn't stop talking with and another with gorgeous blue eyes, Sean. After dinner, a comedy show, and a dance party, Sean got the courage to kiss me. When he did, I responded with the worst response a guy could hope for … I began laughing. He was brazen enough to ask, "What is so funny?"

It felt as if the train going down the tracks of my life had just lifted and changed direction … toward him. I realized in that moment that my whole world had just changed. Sean Hoffmann was the man of my dreams. Sean confirmed my revelation by answering *all* of my questions… and I have a lot of questions. He was better than Google, Cortana, and Siri … and they had not yet been invented.

Sean called me an astral projection because I don't always trigger automatic doors … and because he didn't believe he could get everything he wished for in one person. He proposed in Ireland. I didn't accept his first proposal because, although heartfelt, there was Irish whiskey involved. He staged the second proposal in the most glorious fashion with all the fanciful trimmings … and no whiskey. On one knee, he asked if I would spend the rest of my life with him. I enthusiastically said, "Yes. You asked my father first, didn't you?" He covered his bases.

Nothing alike … and at the same time … everything in common. We were married June 24, 2000. The day after his funeral would have been our sixteenth anniversary.

Together we worked at a medical publishing company that relocated us to Pennsylvania where we pursued the "American Dream" with a house and two and a half children. The half came in the form of our show-winning, adoring, gentle-souled Dalmatian dog Tikka.

As a loving brother and a proud father, Sean realized the greatest gift he could give someone is a sibling. One day he told his adored son Kevin, "Go play with your sister. Oh, you don't have one. I'll make you one." And he did. Well, we did; our beam of light from heaven Rachel. Our children are little replicas of ourselves through whom we experience life from a different perspective.

Sean's greatest achievement was his children. Sean was a detailed observer and a calm problem-solver. With those skills, he could anticipate things before they were an issue. As an example, he cycled through the short list: are they hungry, tired, hot, cold, hurt, need changing, stimulation or love to determine how to bring the baby back to happy.

Sean gladly accepted the tradeoffs required to focus our attention, resources, and affection on Kevin and Rachel. He made the comment, "This will be really hard for about two-and-a-half years, and then it's going to get really good." He was a loving, active participant in raising the children including all the difficult bits. He loved brushing Rachel's hair, playing Lego with Kevin (like building the Millennium Falcon), and working on the computer with both of them. He checked on each of us at night with a kiss; this tradition was termed "Kisstribution." Sean taught them to pay attention to the nuances of their environment as they held clues to what was going on around them. Sean devised complex codes for the children to decrypt and follow like a scavenger hunt throughout the neighborhood. We figured we would expose the children to many things and let them choose their own passion. Sean took such pride in their creativity, imagination, innovation, curiosity, and interest in learning and bettering themselves, and their compassion for others. Kevin and Rachel are his/our legacy.

Intending to build relationships with the family and to prevent the Corvette from freezing to the ground another winter, we returned to California. They welcomed him to the Information Technology Services team at Stanford University which was a dream job. When they could not solve challenges, they sent them to his group of "wizarding unicorn creators." The Intelligence Quotient of this team made the walls bulge. They advanced and innovated. They automated whatever they didn't enjoy doing, making room for more brilliant ventures to support the wisdom held by Stanford. The water cooler conversation included white boarded proofs to determine if the gravity differential would help you jump higher at the equator than the poles.

Occasionally, Sean and I would go to bed with a plan of where in our dreams we would meet up. In the morning, we would compare notes. He would have some fantastic adventure in a gorgeous place; whereas I was saving someone from something or speaking unprepared in front of large, important crowds.

Sean always surprised us with his depth of knowledge and his unique perspective on things. Some things Sean and I loved to share included traveling to learn about other cultures, people, and food. We adventured Ireland (staying at Ballymaloe cooking school), sailed the Greek islands, and enjoyed a wedding and the sunset in Santorini. Because my cousin and his best friend were married on our first anniversary, we shared this celebration in Canada, whale watching. We enjoyed swimming at the cabin in California's gold country and on many beaches. We danced in Puerta Vallarta with friends. On October 23, 2015 the morning after we renewed our vows in Belize, a generous and heartfelt bucket-list gift from our community, I found a handwritten note in my bag from Sean. His words read, "My Dearest Michelle, thank you for being the woman of my dreams for over fifteen years. I wish we could get away a lot more often than once every two years. I am so excited for our trip together. I hope when you read this you know how much I love you, with all my heart, Sean."

A week before his passing, on the evening before the children left for summer camp our family, including Tante Teri, related by love, held hands making a circle of love and shared nice words. There is no explanation for why we needed to lose Sean. There is a need to focus on life, celebrate joys in life and love and laughter. Sean spoke of how he was impressed by the generosity of others. He commented on how developing deep friendships requires the risk of being vulnerable. He is grateful to have made such deep relationships with true friends. He recounted some of the highlights in his life, his friendships and our relationship. He added how it all seemed small in comparison to welcoming the children into this world and how since their arrival he felt bigger, stronger, faster, more powerful, meaningful, and brilliant than he ever thought he could. The children made the difference in the world ... and to him. Kevin and Rachel were so valuable and they were worthy. He said giving up his life was miniscule in comparison to giving them life and making them stronger.

Rachel told me that when she got mad about losing dad, she ran away to the front porch. We may have thought she was gone, but the truth was she was just on the other side of the wall. This is how Rachel chooses to think about daddy: he didn't disappear into nothing. He's just on the other side of the wall.

The path that lies ahead is uncertain. I am not afraid. I have known true love, and it *is* all it's cracked up to be. You know. You are here because you know the authentic love and light from your loss. You know the love for the children and love for you.

The light and love that filled Sean has been released; the world must be a brighter place today.

Honor Your Loved One and Traditions without Grief Paralysis

My daughter was concerned if she moves through and lets go of grief, she will forget her daddy. To help hold memories for her, and free her from grief holding her too tightly, I put together photo albums for each of the children that include pictures of us as a family and lots of images of their daddy throwing them in the air and catching them, playing with them, laughing with them, experiencing life, and teaching them, helping them, and holding them. It's not the same as the real deal, I know. Whether they remember or not, they should know their father was real and he really loved them. That is the message to help prevent grief paralysis. My son honored his father while he was alive and wrote his feelings out once he had passed.

We continue to highlight life celebrations. Maybe the little cap and gown were a bit much for an elementary school graduation, but with a letter of inspiration from their dad, they know their parents are proud of them for this accomplishment. Again, I don't think the majority of us remember every moment of our lives. We do integrate the feeling associated with events that layer by layer create our resilience and outlook on life. If you want to hold the relationship with your late husband, the father of your children, in a good place then that is where he remains. Death is a big life event to survive. I went to four funerals the week of my husband's passing. That was more than enough black and tears to wear in a week. As we acknowledge life's highlights, including the valuable life someone has lived, it is worthy to remember to celebrate the notable events, from something as simple as the magic of the light passing through the leaves of the trees or a touching moment shared with a loved one to a significant life event like a wedding and welcoming of new people into the world.

Often, we don't have the opportunity to share our thoughts with those we leave behind. There is no word in the English language that represents when a loved one is comforting you for their loss. Here are a few of the letters my late husband wrote to the children in hopes they may encourage you as well.

Loving Letters to the Children

For the Days after I Am Gone

Please be open with your mother and tell her how you are feeling. Speak your truth so you can all go through this together. I say go through because it is a process, and it is a path you must walk. You can get through this … together.

I love you with all my heart and then some, for always and forever, near and far and close. Now we are far. I am glad you are in my heart and that you came into my life for always and forever. You have given me purpose, *raison d'etre*, my reason for existing, and more joy than I could have imagined in my life. Now I am gone. You are my legacy. You live on for me, so I will live forever through you.

Take part in life fully. You are extraordinary and I will be with you in your heart. You can do it. Your path ahead is uncertain. It is for you to walk. It is not scary. There is nothing to be afraid of. I have walked my path and I do not see a place where fear will be present or help you. Leave fear behind and walk forward with confidence.

Don't rush your life. Don't grow up too soon; welcome the changes life has to offer you. Growing up is hard. It is worth it. It rarely feels like it is worth it. It is. Sometimes you just have to wait out the low times, the challenges, the storms. You have the strength to wait it out.

Think of me. Think of all of me. I love you wholly and without end. I loved hearing you, seeing you, holding you, caring for you, learning and playing with you. I loved growing with you. You gifted me the opportunity to be the person I was. Not perfect. But, authentic and true.

Little by little over the last several years, we've been handing over responsibilities of your lives over to you, maybe not as fast as you wanted us to, but we didn't want to overwhelm you. We wanted you to see that when life is taken as a series of small challenges; it is totally doable. It is okay to cry for days. It is okay to yell. It is important to release your feelings and emotions. Write it out, draw it out, talk it out, sing it out, write a movie about it, paint your emotions. We hope we have given you the tools to express your feelings in a constructive manner.

I wish I could snuggle and hug you. I wish I could hold you and make it okay that I am not by your side. Know that I am with you. I am proud of you and you make my life meaningful. There are a time and a place for things. These first few days after I am gone are for you to go through your emotions and start accepting that I am gone. I am still with you in your heart ... always and forever.

One Month after I Have Gone

Please remember I am always with you in your heart. I am missing you as much as you miss me. It is time for you to carry on with your normal life and accomplishing your everyday activities. Please put the extra effort into your homework. Your teachers want you to succeed because they know how important doing well, now, with this work will help set you up for success. Like Tikka, (our dog who gave us an opportunity to establish traditions when losing a loved one) all I want is for you to be happy. Please be happy even though I am not here to remind you. Sing and have a light heart, for that is where I will stay.

Six Months after I Have Gone

Thank you for letting me be such an important part of your life. I didn't want to go. I didn't want to leave you. But I have and it is time for you to move forward through your life.

One Year after I Have Gone

It is time to move on now. You must stand on your own feet. You can rely on your family to hold you up. It is time now to move on.

Life in Reverse

How guilty did I feel? How exhausted did I feel? I was a deeply loving caretaker for years and I did not want to leave my lover's side for a moment. Not that anyone would cover for me because they didn't want him to die "on their watch." And when I could be present no further, I would lie down depleted and wonder when, if there would be relief in/after the first year of widowhood. I just wanted to get that first predetermined to be terrible year over with so I could live my life again. I didn't want to lose him. He didn't want to go. The limbo in between was tender and sweet and painful, so painful for him. The day before he passed, I hugged him to help him get up. Mid-process, there was a gorgeous moment that felt like we were dancing, like the first day we met... in the serendipitous day on a cruise placed at the wrong dinner table and the wrong dinner seating. The lively conversation brought Sean to a quick revelation that he met exactly who he was looking for in a woman. We met later that evening on the dance floor where we danced and he kissed me for the first time ...With that kiss, I knew my life had changed. The song *It's in His Kiss* was accurate. This last dance reminded me of our first dance, and the dance at our wedding, and the dance in the kitchen, and the dance with our children, and the dance to just say I love you and am grateful to be in your arms as we share so much of life together. I realized on this day it may be our last dance. I breathed in and held the moment as long as I possibly could, knowing I would have to exhale at some point. At some point, I would have to let go ... but, with my eyes closed and my love in my arms, it felt perfect.

Just a moment in time to be present and experience everything at once. It was a good dance.

And then I embarked on a dance of my own.

Once again, it was my ability to plan ahead and work-life backward that re-stabilized the children and me. I've thought of myself as living traditional values as a wife and mother, I've always set my goals high, reached beyond my comfort zone, and taken initiative to live my best life. I was content sharing that in a partnership. There is no exact right moment to make the decision and start taking action to make changes, big or small, if they are needed to make everyone's lives better/happier. Initially, the only fixed things in my life were the privilege of raising my two children and caring for myself to ensure I could do that. Pretty much everything else was flexible. Eventually, changes in living, career and schools would be made. To ground myself once I accepted that my late husband was not coming home from a business trip and it really wasn't just a nightmare, I prepared for my passing by updating my will and addressing the other legal and financial things required when someone dies.

With that in place, it freed me up to be grateful for having had my late husband in my life and begin the journey through the grief of his loss, living my life, guiding the children forward. One way we honor his legacy is by following his wishes and moving on.

As I regained my energy, I built my inspirational and Subject Matter Expert Advisory Board, the people I rely on for advice. I set health and self-care goals, which I then implemented and celebrated. Setting them and taking the daily steps to accomplish them are wildly different action items. I addressed how I parent the children. The children and I evaluated their strengths and how to capitalize on them, their weaknesses, and how to compensate for them, opportunities, options and obstacles that stand in their way to achieving their hopes and goals. Together, we set paths customized to each child's needs, changing their circumstances from not surviving well to thriving on success trajectories. For myself, I considered different career and revenue income options, re-evaluated my personal relationships and where people fit on what I call my Relationship Spiral. I project managed and layered our entire set of goals, prioritized and focused energy on the children and myself to ensure we are on a path to living a full and happy life.

So, what do you do? You sit down and figure out what you need in your life. And you make sure you don't waste your life energy on things that don't make a positive difference.

Is Grief Gripping Jennifer in the Present or Is She Ready to Take on Her Future?

You are forever changed, and how you approach the next segment of your life will influence the legacy you create for yourself and the children. You need not do it alone. I could not help but reach out to stand by the side of my late friend's wife as she regained her balance in life as head of household and sole parent. Others reached out for me to help them re-evaluate their lives, when they too had lost their husbands, positioning them as the head of household and the only person responsible for their children. As widows and sole parents, you are responsible for everything: walking through the logistics, legal, financial, and emotional issues you may face, and the psychology and neuroscience of moving through grief and moving on. It is natural to think about all the things that might be and all the things that will not be.

Jennifer was challenged to look up to what was ahead of her on the path or in the future in the walking exercise. She just couldn't do it until she was ready. She said things like, "I can only look a step ahead; I don't have the bandwidth for anything else. Even if I try, I get derailed. Because I could plan and plan, and then I have a girl scout troop of children I am responsible for on a field trip to feed the homeless, when suddenly my daughter needs a visit to the emergency room and I've been driving up and down the same main thoroughfare picking children up and dropping them off for the past five hours... oh, and somehow I am expected to have everything on hand to put together a healthy dinner, when all I have the energy for is fetal position in tears. Where is the back-up?"

As she gained her strength, Jennifer realigns her thoughts and activities to future endeavors reducing the time she spends ruminating on the past and feeling lost in the present. She realizes that most of her time and emotions are stuck on being a widow. As she is ready for new developmental stages of moving on from the loss of her husband and standing on her own as head of household and sole parent, she realizes that less of her energy is spent grieving the loss and more of her life is spent in the direction of where she wants to be going, with her head held high, vision slightly above the horizon, with clear peripheral site of her present, where she is placing her feet with intention, what is going on in her periphery and where she is headed into her future, all with an open airway to take a deep breath in. Let's project manage this thing!

The future is coming your way whether you do something about recreating your life the way you would like it, or not. You know better than anyone what is right for you and your children. It's not that you are not smart enough, strong or brave enough. It's not that you aren't resourceful, financially savvy, loving, energetic, or creative enough. You've experienced a major life-role change. You are on the rebuild and you're figuring it out. You are moving toward creating the legacy you are choosing with the conscious decisions you make to be the person you wish to become and support the children along the way.

A Clear Path with the Light Shining the Way

Forgiving is … well, it is for giving. It is forgiven. It is no one's fault. He is free from the pain of being strong for us. We were forced to allow him the freedom to "let go." We will continue on better for having had him in our lives.

I woke up on the anniversary of my late husband's passing hoping for the clouds to part and the light shining on a clear path. It was just another day… without him. I realized that waiting for the first year of widowhood to pass wasn't enough to rebuild my life. There was no set date as to when it gets easier. I had to take action. Almost every decision was easier to align and implement once I could determine whether it would get us closer to our ultimate goal… or not. Simple. Well, much simpler.

Things change. The shape of who we are changes as a result of the choices we make and the events that occur in our lives. It is our gift in life to make choices, including the choice of how we respond to our circumstance and events that happen in our life. Life is not fair. Some of it is hard. We do things that are hard. We know plenty of hard. I had to reevaluate most everything. Were we in the right living situation, academic environment, community and career? I even changed how I dress because I couldn't reach the zipper on the back of my dress or clasp my necklace. (As a stop-gap I used this as a learning moment for Kevin. I asked him politely if he would help me with my zipper and once he had helped me, he was to say, "You look very nice in that dress." Kevin did exactly as I instructed, including the compliment. I fell for it. In fact, I fall for that compliment every time.) Everything came into question. I felt as if I considered everything to establish a vision that is aligned with what is right for our family.

All along this unthinkable journey from our ordinary world, I wondered where the trustworthy, approachable person like me was, who shows up as the mentor to say, "Hi, my name is Michelle. I have experience in this situation and I will be your guide." In situations like these, it is hard to know what to do and where to find the energy to do it. My community saw that I went through loss and rebuilt a life worth living, so they called on me to guide others through the process. Initially, I wondered how I was qualified for this role. As I called on my years of professional and personal life experience, I shared my insight and guidance with those ready to take action and discover their own life worth living after loss. With that knowledge, I could help others leap the hurdles to navigate widowhood and sole parenting. Now that I've figured out that structure and helped others implement it successfully, I have put it here in this book for you.

As I looked for ways to continue to support myself and my children on their trajectories, I woke one morning realizing that I should either redouble my job search to multiple jobs, marry wealthy or write a practical, compassionate guide to expedite the gauntlet I had successfully gone through to build a business supporting others on their journey. One of my sayings is, "You don't always know when it is wrong, but you know when it is right." As I came to this decision, it was as if I had hired myself for the right job. The more people I helped, the more my path opened up and the light was shining on it. I wish no one had to join this club. I am here if I can help you or someone you care about.

CHAPTER 3:

Vision, Align, Implement

"In the middle of difficulty lies opportunity."
— ALBERT EINSTEIN

Much of our life is written for us. Now it is your turn to write your own story. When I was a kid, we played a lot of imaginary games. I called my favorite game, "What do you want to be? I want to be a…" It was an opportunity for each of us to try on different roles and careers and play them out. I didn't realize I would be playing the game my entire life. Now, I can help you play.

You have been rocked by tremendous changes. The events that happen in our lives do affect how we select our steps. Losing your husband changes your role from married to single, partner to on your own, and co-parent to sole-parent, head-of-household, and master decision-maker. Before you met your late husband, you held this role and what has changed is there are more responsibilities, children included. Your role does not define you. That's not all of who you are. A partner does not define or control who you are either. You have done this before and you can do it again.

We are taught how to acquire things in life; not taught how to let go. However, it is imperative to re-envision your life in its new format. You were building a family and a life together with your husband. Now it is your "opportunity" to continue what you built with your late husband. Have you accepted that he is not coming home for dinner? Do you hold any blame for his loss? It will not serve you. Let go of any responsibility for his huge heart giving out before you were ready to set him free. He did not wish to leave you and all the responsibilities left in his wake. Are you ready to stabilize and rebuild your life as he would wish for you to do? He would wish for you to carry on and he knew you could totally live a full and happy life, even though he is not available to share it with you as you planned.

Things Will Never Be the Same

Now what? Things will never be the same. Realize grief is notoriously unpredictable. Assess how it may be holding you back and how it is supporting you.

You have stepped up and taken so much responsibility that you happily used to share with your partner. Accept and forgive. Acknowledge and accept where you are at in life, forgive yourself for not being perfect … there is no such thing.

Give yourself time to adjust to your loss and be sure the changes you're envisioning are in line with your authentic self and do reflect the decisions you want to make.

Vision, Align, Implement

It seems I tried everything to discover what to do and what not to do when navigating widowhood and sole parenting. I charted my process to focus and expedite your experience. I've included stories of others I've helped, like Jennifer, along the way to confirm this process is streamlined and effective in creating a new vision for your future by realigning your authentic self and implementing realistic actions to project manage your life worth living.

First, you will discover a vision to stabilize and support yourself and the children by building an Advisory Board, maintaining your assets, strengthening your health and self-care. Next, you will learn to align your authentic self with your vision to advocate for your children as a sole parent, ensure you have your career, resources, and revenue in place and recalibrate relationships to help others and yourself understand where you and the children fit as part of something bigger than yourselves. Then you will understand how to balance those two support systems by implementing fun/recreation and keeping energy to ensure you are navigating widowhood and sole parenting to a life worth living.

CHAPTER 4:

Who Is Looking out for You?

Want a board of experts looking out for your best interest? How about invested advisors who will look out for the best interest of your children? Those are the people in your Circle of Trust. This is how to develop your Circle of Trust within your Inspirational Advisory Board on your Inner Circle, within your Relationship Spiral.

Your Inspirational Advisory Board is the support system you install around you from the people on your Relationship Spiral, which I will explain. You do not live alone on this planet and one of the most basic ways to ensure your success is to build relationships with a strong network. Connections with Subject Matter Experts, Emotional Champions, Accountability and Network Partners are those relationships that will help you find and maintain your focus along your path in life. These are the people who will support you and have the expertise to connect and springboard you to where you need to be next and they will leverage their position, time, and resources to help you get there. In the process of understanding who is on your Inspirational Advisory Board, you will realize that you have been, are, and will be an Advisor on others' Boards.

It is impossible to be everything to everyone, all the time. You've already shown you have superpower skills by getting to this point. It is vital to replenish your energy for when you need to use your superpowers. Utilize your superpower skills to gain support, delegate and prioritize. What I've learned is that when you have the right advisement, training, equipment, tools, people on your team and realistic expectations of what can be accomplished by when, just about any goal is achievable. I remind the children to use finesse rather than force to get a job done. Occasionally, mechanical advantage using force will make something plausible that finesse doesn't. Don't keep devoting energy to a situation if it is preventing you from moving toward your goals. Adjust your course and enjoy the journey.

One Person Cannot Be Your Everything

To expedite the success along your journey, look for guides. People can only offer what they represent. The middle school Principal can only sell what the public school has to offer. The banker can only sell instruments offered at that bank.

I had an adage, "The more I loved my husband, the more I needed my girlfriends." One person couldn't be everything and everyone to me. That is too much responsibility for one human. My late husband did, however, fill many roles that I look to others' expertise to satisfy now that he is not available. As an example, the children need positive role models. It takes time, and you will find the right role models to act as surrogates and fill in the gaps. For our family, there are people who step up and take one or both to lunch, a movie, rock climbing, on adventures of their own or help with homework. I cannot be everything to them. I have learned to expand our portfolio of guides to offer a variety of skills and not rely too heavily on one person.

Your Relationship Spiral Clarifies Where People Fit in Your World

Imagine you are the center of a spiral. Everyone you know is somewhere on this spiral with those you rely on the most creating your Inner Circle. Who would you put closest to you? This is your Inspirational Advisory Board. There may be people you consider close to you in the Inner Circle, although you don't connect with them as often as others. It is not how frequently you connect with these people or how blood-related they are that determines how close or far away from you on the spiral they are. It's about the depth of connection you have with these people. Those close to you in your Inner Circle who you value and rely on determine your Inspirational Advisory Board. You may have had a best friend in third grade who you relied on completely, but haven't seen since then. That friend was on the Inner Circle back then. Now, however, they are most likely further out on your Relationship Spiral. Not because you don't care, but because they are not in your current Inner Circle. You may connect with them on social networks or get annual updates, but that is probably not the person you call today for mentorship, an emotional refuel or camaraderie. If you reconnect with this person and your relationship picks up where you left off, with the three most important components of a relationship still strong: communication, respect, and trust, then welcome them back to the Inner Circle.

Choose who you hold close, wisely. You may think a colleague is in your Inner Circle, but assess whether this person is a conduit communicator, someone who shares everything you say with the world, especially if it raises their social status to share your information, or an endpoint, someone who can differentiate public versus private information and can keep your personal information, private. Where on the Relationship Spiral are the people who make up your Inner Circle which includes your Inspirational Advisory Board at this time? At the heart of your Inspirational Advisory Board is your Circle of Trust.

Your Circle of Trust

As noted, your Circle of Trust is the network of people (and animals) you reach out to for "relatively" unconditional support. You can develop your Inspirational Advisory Board from anyone on your Relationship Spiral. Deep reliability and trust in a person are what merits the honor of being in your Circle of Trust. There will most likely be people in your Inner Circle who, although they mean a lot to you, may not be a member of your Circle of Trust. Determine who these people are and who you go to for what.

Building Your Inspirational Advisory Board

Adjusting identities is a perfect time to revisit and secure your Advisory Board. Ensure you are accessing the right people at this point in time of your life, particularly at such an emotional time of transitioning from wife to widow, co-parent to sole-parent. The first group on your Advisory Board you might want to reach out to and acknowledge are your Emotional Champions.

Emotional Champions

There are two types of Emotional Champions on your Inspirational Advisory Board, those who listen and will always be on your side and those who will challenge you to be your best and not rest on your laurels. These are the people who support you emotionally.

I wish everyone a friend you can call to rant about any slight the world has disparaged upon you and that friend will agree that everyone else is wrong and you are right. That is a true friend. True blue. You've got a shoulder on which you can dump anything and somehow you will always be right and the rest of the world should do it your way because your way is fun. An Emotional Champion who is a great listener is a great friend to have on hand when you need an ally… or a personal reference.

Look to the second type of Emotional Champion to challenge you in a supportive way if you need someone to be a sounding board with your best interest in mind or put the mirror of the world up for you to face. Although it sounds wonderful to know it all, all the time, sometimes you will benefit from a second opinion that is not your own, to consider all options of a situation, especially if, other options may not be your first choice. I ask if I can talk through an idea or project with these people. It is difficult to be schooled, corrected, or gifted a perspective adjustment, but this type of chiseling hones your skills, expands your boundaries and you get better outcomes.

If you are looking for guidance or support on higher emotional concepts, it may be prudent to invite a professional emotional advisor such as a therapist or psychologist. If you are seeking advice in an arena that is not emotion-based then Subject Matter Experts are definitely the way to go. Again, make sure you are spinning the hot water tap for hot water and the cold one for cold. Go to the right source for what you need.

How Can You Have All the Right Answers?

Subject Matter Experts are the people you call when you need help on a specific topic. You will need to update your will and designate beneficiaries. You can do this for free using tools available on the internet or you may have an attorney assist you. A financial advisor may guide you through investment options. A nutritionist may help you with healthy food recommendations. You may need to interview several people until you find the chemistry, communication, and respect you need to trust someone with these important aspects of your life. If you don't have a master craftsman in your life for whatever it is you need, go find this person. Ask friends and colleagues for referrals. Ask for informational interviews. Write letters to the masters in their field to give you insight into whatever it is you need. And when you find them, listen and follow their advice, you've been given the guidance, take it and act upon it. Commit to investing in your worthy future and the success of your children.

There are several areas in which I've found Subject Matter Experts and followed their lead since my late husband passed. People who excel in their craft hire coaches to ensure their success. Why not me? I lost my partner who I collaborated on all these things. I needed to find experts to fill in the gaps: the attorney, the nutritionist, the Pilates instructor, the half-marathon coach, Beth and Guy Kawasaki, and Dr. Angela Lauria of the Author Incubator. One of my friends pointed out how she was impressed with how I am investing in myself and the children. I didn't understand because I thought I was just filling in the cracks where the light shines through due to my missing husband. This changed my view on how I am choosing to conduct my life.

I felt as if I had a choice of doing nothing and ignore or address issues as they arose, do something which may have mixed results or deciding on what the right thing for each of us in our family was to do. I researched options and selected the best long-term winning solution for the very highest priority items. A very tricky decision was where to put the kids in school. It seemed obvious to place them in the local public school. For a variety of reasons, it wasn't working for my two children. I started with the 'do nothing' option because these are great, local schools. The children did what they could in the situation. It became increasingly clear that although the school is perfect for most, it was not a perfect situation for my children. I didn't want to believe this for many reasons, including it being the school I attended. The game changer was actually a game. As we were taking a walk together, I asked Kevin if he would play along and tell me what my day would be like if we were to switch roles and I was to go through my day as if I were him. Understanding what he endures each day from his perspective, clarified why he was not feeling like this was a supportive learning environment. Playing the game with Rachel had a similar result for different reasons. I realized I had to do something. The school made an effort to adjust the situation but it wasn't enough to transform my children's overall academic experience. I researched and evaluated every option I could consider which resulted in placing each child in a school that is exactly the right environment for their unique circumstance. The positive result of aligning each child in their right environment was immediate. In addition, the Directors of these schools are experts in their fields and have become supportive advisors and mentors to me and the children, who are feeling more secure they can be themselves and pursue who they wish to become. Those were not obvious decisions. I feel confident they are the right ones. The extra bonus is the children are demonstrating they are more resilient and independent with these additional guides to rely on. That was turnkey for me to focus my attention on my next steps. I found experts who showed up for me, who helped me make my next career decisions. Investing time and energy on the highest priority aspects of my life showed me not only how to avoid minimizing my life to just get through it, I feel confident the children and I are making something of ourselves to contribute positively to the world and creating a legacy.

Who Will "Show up" for You?

The car mechanic may be totally capable of fixing your car, but not as sensitive to your feelings about the car needing to be fixed or your feelings on the bill for fixing the car. Your emotional support people are most likely not the same as your Subject Matter Expert go-to people. You may find accountability and network partners overlap other areas. These are people who are advocates and who have your back. They may be the ones who, although they may not have the specific expertise you are searching for, may connect or refer you, using their reputation to help you get your "foot in the door" to introduce you to just the right resource to fill the need.

As my late husband was on hospice, it was difficult for me to leave his side, mostly because I didn't wish to and also because no one else could handle the responsibility of the role. However, one hour a week I would leave to take a barefoot dance class that was a similar class to one I taught a decade prior. I was in the back of the class, trying to keep up while dancing my emotions out and crying. I thanked the teacher at the end of the class and let her know it was the best hour of the week. At some point, I explained that comment. The teacher was compassionate. After three years of dancing in the back of the class there came a day when the teacher was out and the substitute didn't show up. The other dancers in the class knew I had previously taught and asked me to teach the class. I danced with these people. I had not led the class. I had no music. I had no choreography or anything prepared. I had not taught in years. Taken off guard, not prepared, not sure … Sure! I'll teach the class. I turned around to face the group, took a deep breath and taught the class acapella. They had such a wonderful time that when the teacher went out on leave; she invited me to sub her class. I put together choreography and taught the class to an effervescent group. The other people in the class and the teacher were my champions, encouraging me back into a position of leadership and strength. It doesn't make it any less challenging to do the work, but it is empowering to know there is a support group pushing you out of the nest to the next accomplishment.

Accountability Partners are those people who you "show up" for and who show up for you. My children are my Accountability Partners because they will keep me on schedule. Accountability Partners are particularly insightful when it comes to setting priorities, achieving work-life balance, and not losing sight of your values. It is imperative to align your actions toward your goals in line with your own value system. Your Accountability Partners will help you stay on track.

Invitations to Your Elite Inner Circle

There are so many times when people authentically wish to help but don't know what to offer so they make a blanket statement, "Let me know how I can help you." Often, they actually mean it but they don't know how they can offer actual, helpful help.

Here is how to get the right help:

1. Identify specific help you need
2. Be specific about how you will best receive it
3. Show gratitude by thanking the giver and pay it forward when you are able

Gratitude Grows in a Forward Motion

Interestingly enough during my late husband's fight with cancer, after a day of issues at school and moving apartments I lay in a bunk on a cruise (gifted by a friend to enjoy life). I couldn't sleep so, rather than counting sheep, I counted the blessings gifted by people. The words that literally went through my head were, "I wonder what I could do to give back." A booming voice from the dark instantly provided me with an answer. The captain had awakened the entire ship requesting any guests with the right blood type who may be willing, go to the infirmary to help a passenger in critical condition. My husband's smile lit the room, and he suggested I take the extra moment to put on clothes before I fled the room to offer my help, without a moment's thought. It is more often that you cannot "give back" but you can give forward.

If you can figure out the giver's superhero skills and invite them to use them. They will be happy to share their time, skills and resources, and you won't be taking more than they can offer. Does the giver know how to sew or cook? Then invite them to sew or cook. Do they know finances, home repair, how to rearrange the living room, how to walk the dog, teach the children something, babysit, give rides, be an emergency contact? These generous people are actually asking you to highlight their expertise so they can share it with you. This is tremendously difficult, especially when you are sad and lost and no one has made you a coffee or warmed your feet at night. And still, this is a really great way to get the right help for very specific projects.

Then, how do you thank them? I am so grateful to our community who literally kept us afloat, and although I am grateful to all, I am certain I missed formally acknowledging people. People shared what they could with us. For some, that was a real stretch and they did it, anyway. I appreciate any and every gesture as an incredible gift.

To describe this pay it forward mentality, consider the water that runs into a lake and later out to the ocean has been changed by its journey. It cannot send recognition to the source, it can only fill its destiny moving toward its future.

Asking the right thing of the right person at the right time is where things will or won't happen. The key is to figure out other people's bounties. Do they have a plethora of knowledge to share? Do they have a lemon tree that is overflowing? Do they love animals and have time in the morning and need an excuse to get out and walk your dog? Are they great at communicating with children, especially in transit to an activity the children enjoy? Some of the best conversations are from the back seat. Are they already taking their children that way?

You may not get as good a result if you are asking a busy person who commutes to work to walk your dog. These are the people who may be able to pick up takeout on their way home from work as they may be doing that anyway.

It may benefit you to create what we called a "honey-do" list of things that must get done, need to get done, and would be great if they got done. Then see if you can find someone on your Relationship Spiral who has the capacity to get something done on the list ... or get help from or hire the right person for the job so you can move on to the next most important thing you need to address in life, as you are making space for what is to come. My mom had a list of qualified go-to people so we knew who was accomplished at doing what. That help was helpful.

I really don't think everyone expects a thank you note for attending a funeral these days. It is not a situation where a mourner needs to pour their heart out in a letter. With that said, it did build relationships when I did have the energy to cry my guts out in a personal note to people who showed up any way they could.

I have learned that there is strength in being vulnerable. As a giver, it was difficult for me to learn to accept gifts. Even being in a vulnerable state, there are gifts to be shared.

The key to successful prioritizing and delegating is selecting the right person who has the skill and availability to do what needs to be done in the right time frame, with grace. The next important thing is to show gratitude with the three-point thank you. Not that I don't think you know this already, but sometimes having an outline helps the children with some structure.

Three-Point Thank You

1. Thank you for X.
2. X is significant because.
3. How X will benefit us. Thank you again,

Migration on Your Relationship Spiral

You can't get milk from the postman is my friend's advice. It is a clear example of explaining that people can only sell what they represent. If you go to the bank, they will talk to you about how to save or invest your money. You wouldn't think to get medical advice from your banker, or the other way around. Asking the right person for the right thing is an art that requires practice and a bit of finesse. It is also important to note that there are times when your Advisory Board Members fulfill their roles and responsibilities on your board and as much as you may respect, appreciate, and adore them, they may need to be furthered out on the Relationship Spiral … perhaps for another time. Your Inspirational Advisory Board is as changeable as the situation in which you find yourself. Sometimes, it is appropriate to free people up allowing space for the next right fit. The trick is to know when to stick and when to move on. The secret is to be gracious by acknowledging how they helped you. The best way to understand this is to have someone communicate how you were able to help change their life in a positive way.

Acts of Kindness Make Us Happier

The science of happiness suggests in giving you will "receive." There is one more key component to your Inspirational Advisory Board and that is to realize that you are on other people's Inspirational Advisory Board because, of course, your Circles of Trust are concentric circles. You can mentor others by sharing your natural talents and gifts that come easily to you, so there is not a great emotional, physical, financial cost to sharing your bounty. What are the superpowers you have in such great abundance that sharing them would not only not infringe on your well-being, it would fill your emotional bucket? Mentor others and share your skills as an emotional support, a friend who provides constructive criticism lovingly, a Subject Matter Expert, Accountability or a Networking mentor. Mentoring could mean sharing quality time or any of your skills with others. We were gifted an opportunity to bring, prepare and serve food in orphanages. We brought art supplies to teach origami and paper bead necklaces. We played together and shared a wonderful time. We learned how they create family. Listen for the lessons they have to teach. For me, I love listening to someone's story and seeing the big picture, to help them recognize appropriate next steps to bring them to their dream come true.

Volunteering your time and energy is a way to give forward. Share your talents with the world. Be sure to find a way that suits your personality and circumstances. Do not undervalue the small things, smile, connection or company may be enough. You might have time to share, you may have money or resources or connections to share. You will find the right time and space to "share it forward" so no rush this may not be the time. Beware. I have a friend who occasionally gives more time/money than she has, which puts her in a compromising, overextended situation. That is not the intention. This led to a saying in our family: "Take what you need; not more than what you need. Give what you can; not more than you have."

How Can You Give and Be Everything to Your Children?

Surround yourself and your children with people who love them. If not related by blood, then related by love.

How can you be everywhere and do everything all the time for your children? What is the most important role you can fill for your them? In my case, it is comfort and guidance. We would get tense with each other when doing homework together. This was an area in which someone else's voice was beneficial. I listed out the greatest gaps my children were feeling and found surrogates. A math tutor to help with homework. He is a friendly guy who can explain their school math in a way they could not only understand but relate to. Plus, at the end of fifty minutes, (Don't tell them.) he lets the children win a math-related game to increase their confidence and competence. As a full-time tutor, this could mean he loses upwards of 2,000 games a year. What a guy! A science tutor did experiments with the children which they especially enjoyed because it is something my late husband would have set up and enjoyed.

My ability to be there for the children had diminished. I was sad and less tolerant and certainly less patient. How could I think they were not experiencing the same? So, I decided to prioritize the most important things and leave perfection to other people's families.

There are things that have changed because a family member has passed, every day maintenance and chores is not one of them. The children pushed me into creating two categories of challenges: everyday challenges and because-dad-passed challenges. Cleaning their rooms is an everyday challenge they tried to turn into a because-the-dog-and-dad died challenge... I did not buy that. The debate was settled. Even if there are occasionally Legos all over the floor, Kevin clears a path to his bed so I can safely come in and kiss him goodnight.

Does Your Happy Place Include a Puppy?

How did I lose touch? The root cause was that my husband died and I felt disconnected. I had not realized the huge lack of joy in our lives. I had not noticed my characteristic laugh was missing. I didn't even know I had a "Meow" to lose. It was brought to my attention when my characteristic jubilant energy had returned and the people on my relationship spiral noted my "Meow" was back. I didn't notice touch was completely gone from our family. Until a neighbor made a friendly gesture of putting his hand on my shoulder. I tried to hold it together. It was a friendly, publicly made gesture. He barely touched me, but I had not been touched in so long, except for the occasional sympathetic I'm-sorry-for-your-loss-hug that it was like a sensory overload. Touch was gone. I had not been held or loved by my husband. I hadn't touched my children when they needed their parent's connection more than ever.

Touch is a basic human need. I asked myself what is an appropriate way to reintroduce touch back into our lives? I put an open hand on the children's backs to remind them I love them. I scratched their back as they wound down to go to sleep. I didn't have much bandwidth. It felt forced. Interestingly enough it was getting the dog that brought so much back into our world, including touch.

A dog could be more than a decade of love, money, and time commitment. This is a decision you need to make for your circumstance. If a pet is right for you, find the pet that fits the personality of your family.

We talked about getting another dog. The children wished for a dog similar to the one daddy had chosen. That was a huge request but our big, great news is that, after two years of searching, we found a female, liver-spotted, show-quality (that we don't have to show... the children wanted their dog to have puppies.) Dalmatian! We named her Pixel. We occasionally call her by her well-loved predecessor's name, Tikka. She doesn't seem to mind a bit. She is so sweet. The children may or may not be happy to see me in the morning, at night or when I drop them off or pick them up. But they are always enthusiastic to see the dog. So, I send the dog ahead to wake them in the morning and they wake up in a good mood. When I drop them off, they kiss the dog. They kiss me, too. To add to that, she is teaching us all kinds of things like:

- Pick up your toys and shoes or they may be eaten
- Take the dog outside or there may be a mess to clean up
- Don't leave the front door open or you may need to chase the dog
- Train her... or she will consider herself higher than you in the hierarchy and that is no good for anyone.
- ...and yes just as you think she is adorable when she is sleeping, I think the same of you. (Oh, Mom!)

As we all pet the dog, I remember to "pet" the children, too. We have gotten to gentle, play-roughhousing occasionally, something my late husband did with the children. The children do a wonderful job taking part in caring for their new family member. We have joy and laughter back in the house. That is a big job for a little dog. The dog-shaped hole in my heart has been filled right back in.

Wouldn't It Be Nice to Be the One Giving the Help Rather Than Needing It

Just as it is important for you to realize your value in the world in many ways, including by mentoring others as you are mentored by your Advisory Board, the children need to know how they can add value to their Relationship Spiral. The children can volunteer to help a neighbor, walk a dog, act as a mother's helper, or help an organization designed to offer help at a food kitchen, donation center, etc. Scouting and religious organizations typically have those opportunities built into the programs. We make dinner as a family for other families just as our community did for us. Dinner on the table wasn't on the realm of possibility while we were sitting on the kitchen floor grieving and crying. When a community member showed up with comfort food, it was a miracle.

Life is short. We have re-prioritized everything. It is not important if a glass breaks or the car breaks down. It is important if a promise or a heart breaks. It is not important if sand gets all over the floor. It is important that we went to the beach and played in the sand. It is not important what we do, as long as we do it together.

The items that make the top of the priority list are all about connecting, creating and appreciating precious life-moments. Prioritize, train, delegate, and make quality time with the children, so they remember you value them, and even as you are moving through grief and loss, regaining and rebuilding, they are a top priority.

I sat down with a wise guide who posed challenging questions upon which we continue to ponder and take action. The intense emotion and anxiety of our lives are now strung together with small, medium, and large memorable "life-moments." We know that it is thousands of small moments that chisel the relationships in our lives. These are seasoned and highlighted with the larger moments. Giving the children my full attention in short bursts is the best I could do. It is what they needed.

Even if you tell them you'll give them fifteen minutes to do whatever they want, those will be the most valuable fifteen minutes you remember. I am not saying it is easy to do whatever your children want for fifteen minutes. I'm saying it is the most valuable and memorable fifteen minutes. I spent fifteen minutes "flying" around the playground with my daughter and her friends once as one of the herd of winged unicorns. She was so pleased I would play her imaginary game with her and her friends. Her friends were pretty impressed, too. Those were a valuable fifteen minutes.

Sad, Mad, Glad

I learned Sad, Mad, Glad from my sister. Here is something I wrote about it for the local parents' club newsletter:

Our children's bedtime routine is much like any other family: bath, pajamas, a story, song, kisses, and wishes for sweet dreams. Recently I learned we do something a little different from other families "Sad, Mad, Glad."

Children are full of opinions, ideas and observations and they love to share them, especially if you'll listen. Some families talk about the highs and lows of their day at dinner time. Local families talk about what they are thankful for as they sit together for a meal. And some save this ceremony to discuss "favorite things" as bedtime conversation.

In our house at bedtime, each child takes a turn to talk about something that might have made them sad, mad, and glad through the day. Sometimes, we review what happened throughout the day, in reverse to help them remember the events of the day. We let them say what they wish.

It is often heartwarming to hear about things that make the children glad. My daughter says one hundred million things made her happy each day. She warms my heart with her gratitude for life's pleasures when she is asked to name a few. She notes how much she appreciates family time spent together, a kind gesture her brother made toward her or how a bug tickled her hand.

Initially, I was concerned about revisiting the negative events of the day in addition to celebrating the joys. Actually, it is helpful to visit the challenges of the day when the emotions and heat of the issues are calm. It gives us an opportunity to review challenges the children faced and discuss what happened, why, alternatives and how they might have handled them better.

Through the process I was able to learn that my son was in a bad mood because of something that happened at school. He knew there would be an appropriate and comfortable time to talk about a challenge he faced during "Sad, Mad, Glad." We talked about how he responded and ways he could have responded to the situation and what he could do in a similar situation. He felt relieved to talk through what happened and better prepared as a result of the conversation. I may never have known the issue had occurred had we not established a routine of talking about these things each evening.

Reinforcing the importance of the process, I take the opportunity to voice things that may have made me sad, mad or glad during the day. This gives me a chance to role model for the children. It also gives me another chance to highlight what they did during the day that made me proud and glad.

Through the process of discussing the children's feelings and what made them sad, mad, and glad, I have learned what is important to my children; we build trust and bond as we talk together. I know there will be times when communication is difficult between us; my hope is that "Sad, Mad, Glad" establishes a way to keep communication open throughout our lives.

If ever you find yourself in a leadership position, turn to your most trusted friend/guide and ask what would you do in my situation? Just because you are the leader doesn't mean you don't take counsel. It is also important to remember that a strong leader can allow another to take the lead without losing their leadership role. Do that with intention and guidance rather than giving up the wheel and you will strengthen your team as those who came before you strengthened you.

Identify where people are on your Relationship Spiral. Determine where you may need support, acknowledge your Circle of Trust and build your Inspirational Advisory Board so you are emotionally stabilized and ready to move forward and do the same for the children. With emotional stabilization, you are prepared to ensure you are legally and financially secure to achieve your vision in alignment with your values.

CHAPTER 5:

Ground Rules to Protect Your Family and Fiscal Life

The straightest distance between two points is a line. Prepare the details for when your "time" comes, assess where you are today and you have two points. The rest is enjoying the journey.

When I realized this, I was at a point in which the plans I had figured out for my life and future were cut off because they included my late husband. When you go through something so massively tragic, all the things you hoped for somehow disappear in a snap. Poof. My future felt bleak with nothing to look forward to. I had to develop new plans. Initially, I couldn't think about long-term goals, let alone what would happen that month, week, or even what I could get done that *day*. It was moment to moment and breath to breath. My mind was stuck on the end-of-life details. To bring myself back to the present with the ability to see the future I decided to work backward and address my end-of-life details.

Death is part of life. We plan for the other big four life events: Birth, Rites of Passage like getting through puberty, graduations and major personal life accomplishments, Partnership/Marriage, and Welcoming Children. Plan for death, too.

I planned for my untimely demise. I updated my will. I discussed with and legally designated who will take care of the children and the dog. Even without the details, knowing a plan is securely in place helped the children relax enough to feel confident they are and will be cared for.

I updated my beneficiaries with the bank and planned my funeral so the children wouldn't have to. Then, I made it clear to them that however it rolled out doesn't matter to me. They should do what brings them comfort.

To protect your family and fiscal life, here are some things to establish or update to ensure you have what you need to expedite the process of closing your late husband's estate so you can move on.

1. Navigating Priorities

What do you do now? Depending on your situation you may be challenged in some aspects of your life. It is time to evaluate income, assets, liabilities, the children's needs all with a whole heap of sad sitting heavy on your heart. I get it.

There was an outpouring of promises and support. As one dear friend pointed out, what we need is staggered love. I tried to figure out how to put people on a calendar to check in with us and offer the gifts they have to share over time.

I had solicitors "ambulance chasing" and trying to sell or up-sell things to me. I had to decide not to make big financial or life-changing decisions at that time so I knew I was making the right choices for the right reasons. The phone company was included on this list as they were trying to up-sell me on a new plan because my husband had passed. Ugh.

Doing the right thing right was one of the greatest lessons I learned in business school. It could be that you do the wrong thing wrong, the wrong thing right or the right thing wrong. Understanding how to find the right resource capable of doing the right job is an art. Finding the right resource and Subject Matter Experts to refer to when seeking advisement regarding your legal, financial, health, parenting, career, and relationships is key to navigating toward the target goals you set for yourself.

Priorities have changed. I don't have the patience to spend much time talking, doing or waiting for things that just don't matter. I have seen first-hand that life is too short. Here you are. You didn't choose this path. You didn't study your whole life and earn some credential and upon receiving a frameable certificate you get additional letters at the end of your name adding credibility to the words that drip from your lips. Quite the contrary, on becoming a widow, society snatches away the Mrs. initials at the beginning of your name, reverts you back to the Ms. you were or Miss (Yeah, there is a lot you "miss" as a widow.) You may be exiled from couples' events or politely invited as a rickety third wheel, or worse, pushed to the back of the room with whispered understanding of the tears you may be holding back.

I was even gifted the squint-eyed inquisition when I was happy to see someone I had not seen in a long time, "You are a widow. Why are you smiling?" She successfully wiped any enthusiasm I had for seeing her off my face and I carried on with the best charm I could muster.

Living in our current society requires connecting with and completing paperwork with professional agencies. Despite grief, loss, possible depression, loss of energy, enthusiasm, partnership, future status, and a myriad of unknowns, there are agencies who feel it is vital for you to show up cheerfully to inform them of this massive change in your life. You are responsible for getting these things done.

Maybe you're depressed and can't get out of bed, yet. Give yourself some slack for a bit, but set a limit so you have intentional downtime and a set time to get up, wash your hands and face and brush your teeth, and get your life moving in a forward direction. Sooner or later it is time to make your bed, mostly so you don't get back in it during the day. Clean the kitchen sink. If it hasn't happened already, little by little you will find you can move from functionally catatonic, feeling paralyzed to getting back to, well maybe not back to, but forward to being happy and laughing. Your children need you and they need you to prepare for them. Right now your children need you. You alone are the person to do this. They need you to put your affairs in order. We are not planning on the untimely event of your passing. Planning your future will help alleviate uncertainty in your life and give your children the security of knowing they will be cared for, even if you are not available to them. Because of the loss of your spouse, you know how vital it is to have everything in place to allow those left behind to grieve the loss and move forward, rather than get mixed up with logistics and legal issues.

Now that you've been through this, you know it is a kindness to be prepared. As common as death is, pretty much 100 percent certainty, it's not something we always have organized with everything in place. I decided to work my life backward. I didn't write my own eulogy, as much as some of my loved ones might enjoy that. I put enough of my post-last chapter of life in place that it helped provide me with a sense of stability to move forward again in that direction … no rush.

2. An Ounce of Compassion and Some Easy Practical Steps

People may not understand the widow's way. But we have a different perspective on life. In my case, I saw life in fast forward. It is short and it is up to us to value its sweetness. Maybe we reallocate our time to share with people of value. We may feel quick to emotion, but remember that knowing we don't have forever provides a different perspective and value of taking a breath and seeing things by understanding what we would like the ultimate outcome to be and then working backward to make it happen, whether it is planning a project, dinner, a conversation, a relationship or the logistics of our lives.

One thing to be keenly aware of is that some decisions do need to be made right away. There may be times when you feel like you just want to get through all the paperwork and processing and get on with your life. I call that being "on this side of that." "That" in this case is the logistics of closing things up for your loved one. Then there are days when you would prefer to curl up and hope to wake up next to your husband, holding him, sharing your terrible dream.

People don't wish to address mortality especially when living each day can be overwhelming enough. It is important to communicate with your community, including your employer so they know what is going on with you. Ensuring money is flowing correctly so bills are paid appropriately, like the mortgage, car payments, monthly bills, etc., will provide stability and prevent loss of assets. It could take six months to a year, depending on the complexity of the estate to settle probate.

3. Access Resources and Avoid Losing Revenue

Whatever your employment situation, you've had a reality check on life and that is a reminder to ensure you are living your precious life in the way you wish to live it. If not, evaluate your options and recalibrate your course. Is this the time to reinvent yourself? Is the career you've been in going to serve you and the children to meet your life goals? After evaluating her options, including pursuing her original career as a teacher, Jennifer decided that as the administrator of her late husband's company, she could step up and become the Subject Matter Expert in his place to carry on the business. Being the business owner is a big role change and with it comes new challenges. Be kind to yourself and realize the bumps in the road are there to slow you down and confirm you are still on course.

If you need time beyond your employer's bereavement policy, you may talk with your Health Care Provider to determine if disability is an appropriate option as a short-term measure to take some time to check in with yourself and the children. Unemployment insurance is another safety net that may be of assistance. WIC, Welfare, and Food stamps are all possibilities. It doesn't have to be a forever thing. You may qualify for support until you are back on your feet. Things vary from state to state and country to country.

4. Protect Your Family by Securing Documentation Is Current

Avoid feeling vulnerable. Here are some things to put in order to set up ground rules to protect your family and fiscal life. Although none of this is legal advice, it is intended to be helpful to ensure you have what you need to expedite the process of closing your late husband's estate and securing your life in reverse so you can move on.

Updating the following *does* need to get done:

1. Will – Update your will for wealth preservation and allocation to beneficiaries. My suggestion is that you email them to a trusted advisor, send hard copies and keep a hard copy in a safe deposit box or fireproof safe. Your loved ones need to know where to access that information, so let them know where your instructions are located.

2. If your children are eighteen or younger a key element as a sole parent is to determine who will care for your children. This is another conversation that is difficult and yet vital to have with someone you know who could take on this responsibility, would take on this responsibility and hopefully, would follow your wishes which you should discuss with them and you could make clear in your ethical will.

3. An Ethical Will is not a legal document, but rather a letter of sorts written to your family and friends that shares your values, life lessons, and hopes for the future.

4. Trust – A trust is a legal entity to assign assets and helps avoid probate.

5. Power of Attorney – There are different types of Powers of Attorney. Based on the limitation of their role, Power of Attorney designates people who can speak on your behalf.

6. Advanced Medical Directives – This is a loving gift to help those who love you during an impossible time. Designate someone capable, who you trust to make decisions on your behalf in the event you are unable to make them. Get their approval on this and discuss how they could help make decisions in your best interest. This document answers whether you would continue your life on life support, if it could extend your life? Would it consider the quality of life? What is quality of life to you? Advanced Medical Directives are maintained at your hospital. You could also have them easily accessible where you spend most of your time … and with your will.

To get just about anything processed, you will need your late husband's and any dependent's personal details including:

• Social Security numbers

- Driver's License
- Passport Number
- Birth Certificate
- (If applicable) Marriage Certificate or Divorce Decree
- Death Certificate
- Discharge Papers if the decedent was a veteran, you will need a copy of the decedent's DD Form 214 (Report of Separation).
- Locate member numbers of any memberships in professional, fraternal or military organizations.

It is surprising how many agencies require original copies of death certificates. Start with ten copies of the death certificate from the county clerk's office. To close and transfer accounts, you will need to provide original copies to the following agencies:

- Financial institutions – Check for any automatic deposits/ withdrawals.
- Mortgage and other real estate transactions
- Government dealings – Apprise, fraternal or military organizations. If he was a veteran, get a copy of his DD Form 214, discharge from active.
- Insurance
- Legal representatives, Attorneys & Accountants
- Employer – His and yours if you request bereavement benefits
- Credit bureau and consumer reporting agencies
- Cell phone carrier (Change his message appropriately.)
- Cable, gas & electric companies
- Social media accounts (Post an update. You can memorialize accounts.)
- Frequent Flier mileage

Other benefits that may need to be considered:

- Group life insurance from employers, labor unions, fraternal or professional organizations.
- Insurance on mortgage loans, credit card balances, vehicle loans or other loans.
- Accident insurance
- Retirement plans, either with an employer 401(k) or 403(b) plans or in Keogh or Individual Retirement Accounts (IRAs)
- Review taxes owed by your late husband and the estate.

5. Ensure You Maintain Your Assets

Pull together the following information noting a list of assets, the things you own of value and a list of liabilities, any outstanding loans or bills, to make an assessment of where you stand financially. This will help you determine your fiscal starting point and assist in determining appropriate next steps.

- Personal information for you, your children, and your late spouse. You can add any others who depend on you financially.
- Make a list of real property, furniture, personal effects and vehicles with outstanding loan balance, include license fees for registration, and market value. Detail total value you have in (including online) banks and savings, stocks, and bonds. Include the owner and value of your technology, computers, mobile devices, digital assets (including domain names)/ cryptocurrency intellectual property (copyrights, patents, etc.)
- Deposit paychecks, retirement benefits, social security, and VA benefits, or other income.

- Note who is insured, the cash value and death benefit for all term, whole life, split dollar, group life insurance policies.
- Describe any retirement plans and current value of pension, profit-sharing, HR 10 (Keogh plans provide workers who are self-employed with savings opportunities that are similar to those under company Pension plans or individual retirement accounts (IRAs), IRA, SEP (Simplified Employee Pension), 401K.
- Record any business interests you may have including general and limited partnerships, sole proprietorships, privately owned corporations, professional corporations, oil interests, farm, and ranch interests. Include who has the interest, your ownership in the interests, and the estimated value of the interests.
- Describe and give values for all mortgages or promissory notes payable to you, or other money owed to you.
- Document any inheritance, gifts, or lawsuit judgments
- Payment of state and federal income and property taxes
- Safe deposit box rental fees

Consider whether you think you might benefit from having long-term care insurance?

6. Balancing Income and Expenses

Losing a family member often means losing household income as well. Determine the amount of your living expenses and subtract it from how much you have available each month. Use this information to establish or revise a budget. Adding an emergency fund ensures you have available cash for unplanned expenses, such as vehicle or home repairs or temporary unemployment. It should be enough to cover your basic living expenses for three to six months.

Protect Yourself from Fraud and Identity Theft

Avoid the perils of being vulnerable or taken advantage of during a vulnerable time and get the support you need to restabilize yourself and the children.

- Fraud and identity theft may be the last thing on your mind and that makes you an easy target. Update the appropriate associations as noted. Limit personal information you share in public places like birth date, mother's maiden name or other personally identifying information. Review financial activity and report any questionable activity. You know he is not making purchases after a certain date, so report anything that doesn't look right to you.

Assemble Your Support Team

1. As you are building your Inspirational Advisory Board, there are people you may consider as regulars or even on a temporary basis to help you with the legal issues. You may need an attorney, an accountant, and a financial advisor to settle your spouse's affairs.
   a. If it is appropriate, find the right therapy and/or grief counseling for everyone – group therapy, children's camps, individual therapy
2. Free yourself of things, people, circumstances that don't serve you and find positive role models who can share a similar experience and/or who can also act like a supportive role model.
3. There are groups like Big Brothers and scouting for children. There are camping opportunities designed for children who have lost a parent. It is important to consider if your children are ready to be away from you while engaging in exercises

related to evaluating their feelings about their lost parent. It can be intense. If the leaders of the camp are highly skilled and qualified to facilitate these types of exercises and respond to grief expressed by children, it can be an opportunity for children to move through grief with peers in a similar situation.

4. Social Services

I have heard mixed experiences with some of these groups. You will always be the best judge of who you and the children need in your Circle of Trust.

Before Sarah's husband passed away, no one would have looked at her family through a lens of potentially hurting themselves or others. Protect your family from people who may not understand the emotions your family is facing during a vulnerable time. Sarah is selective about people she invites into her, and her children's, Circle of Trust to ensure her Inner Circle consists of people with the capacity to see their whole picture and listen to their perspective. In their family, they no longer sing song lyrics that relate to death, harm or killing. They don't cite movie references or even colloquial sayings like "You're killing me," "I was bored to death," and "I thought I was going to die I laughed so hard." These are harmless comments until you are viewed as upset because your husband or dad died.

Sarah says, "Things are not my priority. The children are my priority. Our character and integrity have been tried and tested since losing my husband. I realize there are people who need help and that is where social services agencies are very helpful. At the same time, it saddens my heart to know reports are filed, abusing the resources of the agencies, and frightening the remaining family members that they may lose each other." I have heard this with several families. If it happens to you, just know they are checking for your well-being.

When child protective services contacted Sarah, she thought it was to help fundraise for a project she was working on with another agency that protects children. She was incorrect. Child Protective Services invited them into the office where they clearly demonstrated they were a solid and loving family, regardless of the tragic loss of Sarah's late husband.

Other Places to Ensure the Kids Feel Valued

- Family members and friends can be role models who may provide insight your late husband shared. For example, I cannot speak physics and computers with incredible detail. But, a colleague and good friend of my late husband does. My son reaches out to him (and so do I) when the topic is too far above our heads.

- Camp counselors and extended family members can be great surrogates to escort your daughter to the father-daughter dance.

- Another source could be a teacher who could become a soccer coach, tennis buddy or rock-climbing partner.

- Animals provide an unconditional love and they are really good listeners. Horses provide an outlet to gain control over something in life. Both horses and dogs love hearing your children's innermost feelings and thoughts. They make wonderful confidantes and give unconditional love.

- Activities like hiking, camping, traveling, learning to sail provide an understanding of the world around the children and how actions have consequences that can be adjusted to maintain course.

CHAPTER 6:

Health and Self-Care – Not Only Your Life Depends on It

The most important thing you can do to feel safe and secure when loss has rocked your world is care for your health. You have renewed reasons to get it in your control. Your health is of tantamount importance to your success and your children's future.

Prioritize your health as everything else hinges on it. Everything you do, every decision you make should be a choice to reach your ultimate goals. What should you eat? Should you get a good night's sleep? How do you feel secure and calm enough to get a good night's sleep? Should you save? Should you spend? What will be the best use of your precious time? Should you plan for tomorrow? Live in the moment of today? Are you more risk-averse because you are a sole parent? Your children cannot afford to lose you. Make choices as to how you will use your limited supply of energy.

Who Will Take Care of You?

Whether you were a long-term caregiver to your late husband and losing him was a tragedy or you experienced the shock of a tragic loss, you've been caregiving for everyone else and it is time to put yourself in line for some attention before your health slips.

You know how often to check in with your Health Care Providers for your own health needs. The problem is, of course, actually doing it. At the basics, you may want to adopt the habit of selecting a specific week each month and declaring it "Health Week." At least one week of the month pay attention to general maintenance such as: make routine health care appointments, make choices that benefit your long-term physical self to be present for the children today, tomorrow, and for a healthy long time. Do the same for the children.

I am not a doctor. I do not claim to be one or make medical recommendations. The recommendation I am making is to prioritize your health. What I can represent is the importance of acknowledging stress and how you respond to it. Of the many stressors that cause health concerns, losing a spouse is at the top, not only because you've lost security, there are ripple effects that cause stress, as well.

Take Care of Yourself

People say, "Take care of yourself." It is beyond me what it really means. Is it like, "How are you?" I answer with responses like, "I am happy to see you." Or "I am happy to be here." Truths that skirt the social inquiry. Now, I say I am good, because I feel that the children and I are good. "Take care of yourself" is a loving intention wishing you include yourself on your valuable list of people to care for. For every ten things you do for others, you could consider including something for yourself, even if it is a bath or a nap.

I have a friend who loses weight when she is stressed. This is an anomaly in my world. I am of the body type that I cannot lose weight when under any stress. I am more like a puffer fish that expands when under stress. Science suggests that due to increased cortisol in our body during stress it is challenging to adjust body weight. My family has been in life and death stress for years. The advice I do have is to nourish your body in every aspect to maintain resilience and keep going. If you are stabilized and relaxed in most aspects of your life, it will allow you to focus your energy on the important priorities. Understand the importance of acknowledging stress and how you respond to it.

Willpower is a limited commodity and when emotions are in play, it is difficult to make the choice that is in your best interest in the long run. So, again choose your priorities as to where you share your energy and let go of energy zappers. When the time is right … and you will choose this, you will start to make choices that rebuild your energy bandwidth, and refill your emotional bucket.

Good Food-Food

As I face challenges and willpower obstacles I remember when sweet Rachel was very little, she developed the best self-help advice of all time:

Two of Rachel's invisible friends were named, "Food-Food": Good Food-Food and Bad Food-Food. Good Food-Food sets a good example, eats growing food, and has good manners. Bad Food-Food eats junk food, has bad manners, and teaches everyone bad manners. You can try to get rid of Bad Food-Food, but Bad Food-Food is very powerful and keeps coming back. Although Bad Food-Food is very strong; you just need to be a little more powerful than Bad Food-

Food to win the fight. This rings true of every willpower test you face. You don't need to be the Olympic athlete of Willpower. You just need to be a little more powerful than the challenge you are facing to get and stay ahead of it.

Be kind to yourself. Listen to your self-talk and the tone of your inner voice. I had a very loving relationship with my late husband. If his is the voice in my head, my self-talk is reassuring and loving and forgiving and he would say things like he wishes he could be here with me, too. And not to worry about things, especially parking tickets and random stupid stuff. Let go of the stupid stuff and focus on the important things.

At the start of my widowhood journey, I felt as if I stood surrounded by a scorched landscape with pretty much nothing except the children. I was alone parenting my two sensitive, grief-stricken children. It was time to take care of myself. The word that rang through my head was the adjective used by my long-term doctor describing my condition: disheveled.

Duh. I was focusing on way more important things than the superficial. However, it was time for the caretaker to care for herself to remain strong enough not to orphan the children. I had not moved my body for months. The role of being by my dying husband's side was complete. There I was overweight, overextended, over the whole situation. I looked disheveled. I understood that was an accurate diagnosis and it was curable.

With a connection to your Health Care Providers and good health habits in place, consider self-care. Beyond general health and wellness, self-care represents lifestyle choices. It encompasses the role you model for your children in the way you live your life, your everyday habits, grooming, eating, exercise, social life, hobbies, and how you spend your free-time.

A friend mentioned although she was not a runner, she was going to run a half-marathon. I had always wondered why people did that. What are they running from? Now I understand the entire thing differently. I was running to something, something intangible. It was still something. I asked if I could train with her. The first mile almost took me down. The second workout almost took me down. I got a massage, and that seemed to help put things in place. The third workout almost took me down. It wasn't until the fourth attempt that I felt, although difficult, that I could keep working out. Everything hurt. I was out of shape. The workouts took on a different tone for me when I realized my Advisory Board supported exercise as time well spent. Hah! I found an outlet that was approved alone time! Fine. I'll run. And run I did. I ran, and I ran. I ran slower than anyone walks, but I was moving in a forward direction consistently. I huffed and puffed while people casually strutted by chatting as if I were moving in reverse. I had two speeds: slow and not quite that fast. Mostly I went slow. Mile four was the point at which tears came out. Every single time. Mile four tears spurted. I cried them out and kept going. After about four or five miles it is recommended you bring hydration along with you. I purchased a belt that held water, sports drinks, coconut water, and some quick energy snacks. As the mileage continued to climb, I felt as if I was jogging along at a party sipping drinks and enjoying appetizers. It wasn't really that fancy but it's fun to think it could be.

I met up with additional friends at this first half-marathon. I ran, I drank sports drinks, and I ate oranges. I watched the slowest people in the world pass me with a shake. A photographer yelled at me to turn around because I was literally running backward and he wouldn't get a good picture. I was using different muscle groups and didn't care much that this look was not captured for posterity. I probably looked disheveled. But I was doing it. I was a little stronger than the challenge ahead of me.

Crossing the finish line was emotional. I was thrilled I accomplished this tremendous goal … and then I felt alone … so alone. The one person I really wanted to share it with was never going to be available to share with me again. I crossed another benchmark … so alone. With a deep breath, I realized I was not alone. I traveled to this race with a friend and others had joined along. I met up with them at the finish line and we all celebrated the accomplishment together. I was not alone.

There is no expectation for you to run a half marathon. The "take care of yourself" inspiration is that you will get enough good rest that you in your body will be inspired to move in a way you love … and stay just a little more powerful than Bad Food-Food.

Emergency Kit of Self-Care Solutions

Breathe

Breathing is automatic. However, when so much of your life is out-of-control, breathing is something you can gain immediate control of. Breathing refuels and nourishes you on a cellular level. Imagine filling your lungs all the way to the bottom of your lower back to get a deep breath as there is more surface area at the base of your lungs collecting more oxygen to get into your bloodstream. Take a breath to fill the sides of your lungs, front and back as well as on top. A big deep breath is one of the quickest ways to nourish yourself and reduce stress.

Sleep

*"The best bridge between despair and hope
is a good night's sleep."*
– E. JOSEPH COSSMAN

Dear Sleep,

How is it I know how much I miss you even though I am unconscious when you are around? It is like no time passes when we are together. Sometimes we go on fantastic adventures, dreaming of exotic places. Sometimes my dreams are frightening. But it is always better to spend time with you, dear sleep, then not.

It always amazes me that the morning minutes go by more quickly than the minutes required to wait for something.

Maslow's hierarchy of needs puts biological and physiological needs such as air, food, drink, shelter, warmth and sleep at the base of the hierarchical levels within a pyramid. One must satisfy lower level basic needs before progressing on to meet higher level growth needs. Once these needs have been reasonably satisfied, one may be able to reach the highest level: self-actualization. Just as one fluctuates between the stages of sleep, life experiences may cause an individual to fluctuate between levels of hierarchy.

One day after little to no sleep, I got home in time to fall in love with my pillows for seven minutes before the children returned home. Words and exhausted tears fall from my mouth: The children are coming home and all they want is for me to be excited to see them and I am *so* tired.

I worked to climb the hierarchy of needs pyramid to include belongingness and love, family and affection by welcoming the children home, making an after-school snack, and helping them with homework. I was happy to let them continue their Maslow's climb building relationships by playing at their friends' houses. I took the opportunity to rest.

It is no surprise that as of late I have not had much sleep. I pondered a thought. If I had an option to forget this exhausting part of my life and wake up as if it were a dream, with a few scars and some vague explanation as to how I received them, would I choose that option? As difficult as this is, I would not choose to opt out. What would Maslow choose? I feel that the lessons I learn and the emotions I feel as I move through this journey are part of living life and my plan is to experience it, however rough.

As Neuroscience professor Matt Walker has said, sleep is an incredibly active state in the brain and body. Your brain is thirty percent more active in some stages of sleep relative to when you are awake. During deep sleep, the brain cleanses itself of toxins that have been building up during the day.

Human beings are the only species that deprive themselves of sleep. No other species that we see will do this without biological gain. And what that means is that evolution has never faced the challenge of insufficient sleep since the dawn of time. As a consequence, Mother Nature has never had to solve this problem of insufficient sleep, so there is no safety net.

Some things that can help you get a good night's sleep include setting a bedtime. Even if you don't make it to bed on time, you know you've got a goal. Lots of bright morning light, then decreasing light exposure throughout the afternoon and evening is helpful. Of course, the light from screens affects natural circadian body rhythms and avoiding caffeine after midday is helpful. Getting a good night's sleep is rejuvenating. Give yourself the gift of a good night's sleep. You'll feel better in the morning.

Hydrate

Drink water! You are made of mostly water. Keep it that way. Water regulates your body temperature, protects your organs and tissues, lubricates your joints, moistens tissues like your mouth, eyes, and nose, reduces the work of your kidneys and liver by flushing waste, helps dissolve minerals and nutrients to make them accessible to your body, and carries nutrients and oxygen to your cells to name a few of water's important functions.

Affirmations

Mantras keep you moving forward. Some of my famous ones include:

- Say yes if it moves you forward
- You are safe, loved, and not alone
- You are confident, competent, and strong
- You can do this

I got you.

Self-Talk

If the voice in your head is not sending you the right message, then talk to my inner voice. She is forgiving, reassuring and tolerant. Although one day as I was walking. I was listening to my inner thighs rubbing together and I thought, oh gee, this has gotten way out of hand. Flip, flop, flip, flop! Really that is the sound of my thunder thighs? This is terrible! It stopped me in my tracks. The flip-flop continued. Oh my, the friction is still flipping and flopping? What am I going to do to get control of this situation? Phew, it was the woman's sandals snapping as she walked in pace behind me. My thighs were in the clear.

Another important note is to remember not to superimpose other people's judgments into your own self-talk. Anticipating others opinions of you may cause you to worry unnecessarily. As well, you may not be right about their thoughts. Be your own best advocate.

Centering/Movement

I offer you this exercise to find your center. Align your knees in the same direction as your toes. Soft knees, soft ankles. Hips in line with your shoulders, soft shoulders, easy breath. Head in line with your spine. Imagine your pelvis as a bowl with a pearl at the center. Sway side to side like a pendulum and then swing less and less until you find center. Do the same thing forward and back. Melt into center and feel your whole foot on the ground. Imagine you are tethered to the center of the earth. Crown of your head is tethered to the center of the universe. You can move easily on this axis with the stability of this grounded feeling. Movement from center is stabilized movement. This is similar to all the exercises we are doing here to provide you with stability to move with confidence, grace, and ease.

Nature/Earth

Connecting with nature is another way to be grounded. Whether walking in natural surroundings, walking barefoot, gardening, or just soaking in some vitamin D, sunshine. Getting out in the fresh air is a brilliant way to feel refreshed.

Touch

Widowhood hurts. It literally hurts. Physically, emotionally, socially, spiritually. That love was ripped away and it is not coming back. Loss of intimacy, physical and emotional. Touch deprivation. Wanting to be held by the person who is not here. The dog helps because there is always some warm body happy to see you. When I cry, our dog runs across the house to lick my tears. When I wake up in the middle of the night we go nose to nose. It's the best I've got at this time. What is the best you've got at this time?

Touch is lost with the loss of a loved one. Suggestions to compensate for this include hugs with loved ones, playing with the children, we do a lot of back scratches. Massages, manicures, pedicures, and facials may seem like luxuries, but they are legitimate ways to keep a human connection through touch. Of course, petting pets is always good.

The dog brought joy, laughter, and touch back into our lives. We barely noticed how we were not connecting in this way. We just felt loss. The great chasm of the most important person in the world, missing. We were not whole without him. It's not that I had not been hugged by loved ones. There have been many sorrowful embraces that try to offer strength, support, and condolence. That is very different in its nurturing. I had not been touched in a very long time. I went out and got a massage.

We had lost our previous dog to old age prior to losing my husband. The children were very specific about the type of dog they wanted because that was the type of dog my late husband chose. It took two years to find the right dog. My community pressured me not to get a pet. They pressured me to only get a rescue. They judged my choices and commitments. I rose above it and found the right dog for my family. I quickly realized the dog was not a rescue. The children and I were the rescues. The dog brought touch back into our lives. We love petting her. The dog brought laughter back into our lives. She is naturally funny. The dog brought unconditional love back into our lives as well as a sense of responsibility to a family member that helps the children see positivity and hope in life again.

We welcomed the right dog into our family and immediately she brought with her the most frequently stated words in our house,

"Oh, she is so cute." That in and of itself changes everything. How can anyone be so very sad when some little sprite is being so very cute? Plus, she is soft and furry, inviting us to pet her, which secretly reciprocates the affection. That's how I realized not only had I not been touched … but I hadn't touched the children. Oh dear, the children lost their father and their mother hasn't even touched them in such a long time. How lonely for them. So, I would reach out while we were petting the dog and pet them, too. That I could do. It was a start. We are back to hugging and bumping and gentle roughhousing and scratching each other's backs. That took longer than expected and it was a greater loss than any of us could initially realize. Laughter. Oh, this dog is so silly. It was like seeing sparkly stars in a darkened room, the first time I heard laughter from my children. The dog is a friend nearby. We tell her our secrets, wishes and share how we are feeling. She listens to all of it. She stays nearby and is ready for whatever energy level we have to share with her. She gets us outside in nature and in the world, with a walk, a hike, an adventure. She reminds us of the routine of the day and responsibility with her care and feeding. The dog is an exceptional guide available to us at all times … with her whole self.

A Life Filled with Luxuries

Prevent or solve the problem, not the symptom. There are times when budgeting for more nourishing food, things you might consider stress reduction like getting help with household chores or driving the kids around may seem indulgent. When you evaluate some basic needs choices, there are things that may seem like a luxury. However, when you do a cost-benefit analysis, you may be better off making what you previously thought was an indulgent choice. Working with a widow, Ashley, she realized that considering the root issue of needing quick, easy nutritious food was not being solved by responding to immediate symptoms of thinking she should select the cheapest alternatives in the moment to satisfy her hunger. We did an evaluation of the cost of ordering a delivered box of ready-to-prepare meals. It is her preference and would help her eat a more regular, healthy diet. However, it was counter-intuitive for her to make this choice because it seemed indulgent. When she considered the cost of transportation, parking, groceries, storage, preparation, and waste or overeating, she realized that in fact having a nutritious meal delivery was a more prudent option ... and saved her lots of time. Plus, she felt like she was indulging by eating healthy food that was delivered to her.

With stress being a great health risk, it is easy to see why making stress-reducing decisions like getting help around the house or with the kids will be better for you all in the long-run. In the short run, as long as you are budgeting wisely, this support will help you emotionally. For myself, I went a step further and indulged in new running shoes, socks, and a free app for my phone to track my exercise. This was an indulgent activity because I was spending time away from the kids and revenue building. The alone time was great to clear my head. The exercise was good for my body. Committing to the training and achieving the goal of running a half marathon was good for my spirit. It is worth evaluating short- and long-term benefits when deciding what will be in your best interest overall.

Choice 1 – Love the Way You Move

One walk at a time. Little differences make big impacts. Make lots of tiny positive differences. For example, do yoga, stretch, walk, hike, run, swim, bike, strength training. You don't need to be the best at dancing to enjoy dancing. Find some movement in your day. Drink lots of water. Fuel yourself appropriately and design a worthwhile reward.

After training for my first half marathon and running it, the children asked if I would take them to Disneyland. I suggested they should go with their peers. They countered by asking if they ran a half-marathon, would I take them to Disneyland. Yes, if they trained appropriately and ran a half-marathon, they should earn just about anything. That was the inspiration for our new tradition of training together as a family. This was a life-changing adjustment for us. A little effort each day or indulging in a day off meant that over time, we could accomplish so much more. Rachel and I ran together. Kevin crossed the finish line yelling, "I hate you, Mom!" Yeah, it's good he was thinking of me, and by the way, he just ran a half-marathon. The toy store was between the finish line and the hotel. It was a mandatory stop before taking a nap after that major physical achievement. In the midst of lost traditions, running is one thing the children and I do together.

What type of movement do you love? When you are making positive, healthy body changes, your motivation soars.

Choice 2 – Healthy, Mindful Eating

Nutrition is a personal choice. The key is finding the right mix of nutrients that serve you and your body, fueling you for what you need to accomplish. You can be your own science experiment to feel what works for you and how much you need to accomplish what you set out to accomplish. Take the time to acknowledge what goes in, how you feel and adjust to what you eat to nourish your body based on the performance you desire out of it.

Choice 3 – You Are Worth Investing In

Whether it is from the outside in – hair, make-up, nails, clothes, and at least good shoes – or from the inside out – cleansing sleep, water, easy breathing, mindset, and nutrition – it is time to set goals for what makes you feel like you are valuable. Jennifer gained certifications in her late husband's business, becoming the Subject Matter Expert. Widow Linda invested in a social club to make new contacts and expand her network. Ready for romance in her life and weary of social websites, Patricia chose to hire a Matchmaker to assist her in the process of finding romance. Sofia chose private schools for her children because they were barely surviving a public school. They are thriving in a private school. Consider an investment in advancing yourself and your skills based on how it will benefit you and the children in the long run. How will investing in the children propel all of you forward in your life?

Focusing on the Right Stuff

Priorities have changed. After knowing intimately how short life is, do you have the patience to spend much time talking or doing or waiting for things that just don't matter? Eliminate or delegate what is lower on the list but still needs to get done. Assess the most important aspects of your life and focus on those. You will feel stronger and more capable of addressing what you and the children need in the process.

You know too well that you don't get to be here forever. Value the moments and experiences you have in life. Celebrate the moments as well as the day, the pitfalls, and glories. And once you are externally stabilized, ensure your health is in good form and you are modeling supportive healthy self-care habits.

Having everything in place for "after my last chapter" in this life provided me with security and stability to think about continuing forward from this point on. I cannot change the past. I've got my ultimate destination tended to. Now I can enjoy the present and the journey. Your good health and well-being are the greatest gifts you can give yourself and loved ones. So, remember to stay just a little bit stronger than Bad Food-Food.

CHAPTER 7:

Sole Parenting – How Do You Raise Your Children to be Good People?

Together we were his reason for living…and when I am not crying through grief for my loss, I realize the great loss to the children, for they will no longer know how vitally important they were to him. They will know my security and love alone.

…and every day I ask, "How am I doing?"

And I receive the message that I am doing all the right things right.

And then I ask, "What should I be doing?"

And I receive the message that I am doing what I should be doing.

And I ask, "How can I help the children?"

And I receive the message that I should be present with the children.

And I ask, "What should I do next?"

And I receive silence.

So I ask again, "Now what should I do?"

And I receive silence.

So I ask in a different way.

What are my gifts and how can I best utilize them to benefit others?

And I receive the message that I know my gifts deep in my heart... and so does everyone else.

So I ask again, "Now what should I do?"

And I receive the message that I should heal. If I had a more physical injury, others would understand more clearly. It is okay they do not understand. I should allow myself to heal.

... "and what about the children? What can I best do for them?"

And I receive the message that I should be present with the children because they need to heal in their own time, in their own way.

You might find yourself in a quiet place, wondering, "What happens now?" There are distractions aplenty: things to clean, children to tend, communications to be made. Occasionally, there is a moment, a sound, a memory, a taste, or a smell that inspires me to move to a more certain time.

There was a time when the present was so unbearable, I could not get beyond it. Although the future was uncertain, it seemed welcome as it came. In the quiet times, I would wonder what I should do at this moment and in the future that is in everyone's best interest. How could I make sure it moves in a positive direction and the children have and will get what they need?

Others would have me get busy just to be busy. I was worried I wouldn't hear what was being informed in the quiet if I was doing things to just be busy. I felt as if the answers and path should be laid out for me, but the path was not lit. I waited and listened closely. Nothing was clear. It was for me to set and light the path. It was for me to navigate the way for myself and the children.

Your Children Are Going through This, Too

Your children have also experienced great loss. In many ways, they will never know the loss they've experienced because they couldn't know your late husband and all his dreams and desires to participate in being in their lives like you do. Often times, children are not given leeway. People say children are resilient. Because they choose to continue on, doesn't mean moving through grief from the loss of their father isn't a challenging path.

People in their Relationship Spiral, at school, in the community, their peers don't know what to do or say. Sometimes, they say, "I'm sorry." That is enough. Sometimes, they ignore it. That could be enough. Acknowledgment, acceptance, and a compassionate listening ear are a better friend than someone who tries to fix the loss or misdiagnose a triggered mood. It is helpful for you to appoint, speak with and prepare compassionate point-people in your children's community who will be respectful and supportive. Invite the children to help designate who these people might be. You may be surprised at who your children see as confidantes. You can help guide them in the right direction. Listen to the message behind what they are sharing with you and telling you when they share their feelings ... especially when those feelings are less than lovely. They are sharing then, too.

Share your feelings with your children so they can role model how you are addressing and moving through this challenging time to live a full and happy life. Let them know your goals, the action steps you are taking to meet those goals and let them know the work is ... well, *work*. Too often other people's lives seem wonderful and carefree. Everyone has a story and everyone works to fulfill their dreams. And still, remember children deserve to have down-time and play-time. Find moments filled with laughter and joy so those are not lost. Go through your list of favorite things and activities and continue enjoying the valuable things in life, like sharing undivided attention moments with your children. Make it clear they are valuable to you and reassure them you know their talents will make a positive difference in the world without putting pressure on them. Just by being the best version of themselves, they will contribute.

It is responsible for you to vocalize the obvious that nothing they said or thought caused their father's death. It is not their fault daddy died. Death is not like it is in video games where you get lots of chances. Daddy is not coming back. They do not need to fill daddy's role in the family. It is their responsibility to be the best version of themselves they can be.

Children need their Inspirational Advisory Board, their Circle of Trust filled with love, patience, and acceptance. The way we welcome their ability to acknowledge and move through their emotions will help set the path for how they navigate challenges throughout their lives. As I set a clear structure for the end of my life, I reassured the children that I plan on living a long time. In the event of my unlikely early death, it brought them comfort to know, even without specifics, I've designated specific and appropriate people to care for them. They should know they have a back-up plan and they will feel safer knowing who they should go to in case of an emergency, even if it is just that you are not available for a ride home from school.

Whatever their father represented to them, he is not around anymore. The good, the bad, whatever role he played is now vacant. Furthermore, your reaction to the loss is apparent to them. It is natural for children to wonder if they were responsible in any way for their missing father. Clear that up. The situation is not a response to something they thought or did. It is not their fault. As remedial as it may seem, remind them of that. There are other things you may need to clear for them:

- They do not need to step in and fill the role of the missing parent.
- They are not responsible for their father's loss or their mother's happiness.
- They do need to allow their emotions to run all the way through them.
- They do need to step up and take more responsibility for themselves.
- They do need to be the best version of themselves.
- They do need to get involved in the world again, bit by bit. It is okay to move forward and you will understand if they need some additional downtime.
- Make a plan for them including safe, understanding people, and places they can go to at school, in their peer groups and community in the event they need a little space and time for themselves.
- Share some rebalancing exercises with them they can do on a moment's notice like deep breathing, in for a count of seven, out for a count of seven, focus on a happy, comforting thought.
- And discuss comfort tools and things they are willing to go outside their comfort zone for which we call "currency."
- Even in the best of parenting moments, children can only learn what they are developmentally ready to hear. Accept and forgive is the starting point to determine where you can move them to.

Determine who you can be for the children. It is natural for children to have the desire to overcome obstacles. When they are ready, or just before they are ready to take on more, talk about setting up challenges with them. If you establish rites of passage or work together to come up with challenges just outside their comfort zone, they will be focused on productive goals and you will have less chance of them finding their own rites of passage, which may be troublesome. Together the children and I have set leadership, compassion and physical challenges. These rites of passage require consistent effort from the children that stretch their strengths just a bit at a time. As a mother, I respect the effort that is required of you to position the children to put the effort forward to achieve these aspirations.

As I've previously mentioned, you can solve seven primary things the children needed help addressing. Consider their perspective and experience to determine if they are hungry, tired, too hot, or cold, hurt, need something external changed, stimulation or love. Using these as a point of reference is a helpful starting point to figure out how to best determine how to listen, guide or help them. As the children mature, so do their challenges. And still, ensuring these basics are in place provides them, and you, with more stability and focus to address the more complex issues. As they grow, you can designate the responsibilities they can take on as individuals.

If the children can take some responsibility for themselves that gives them a sense of control in their lives that is developmentally appropriate and allows you to be a role model asking for what you need, the children should learn to be specific and do the same. Of course, they still need boundaries.

How Can You Be Both Father and Mother? – Communication, Trust, and Respect

Love is powerful and loving another is the most vulnerable and humbling joy life allows you to experience. Super fun adventures, good chocolate, and gorgeous smelling flowers rank high on the list, even those are experienced more intensely with love. Just as in other relationships the three most important things are communication, respect, and trust. We have a saying in our family, "We tell the truth, even if it is hard." We mean that we will always back each other up. We need to know we are there for each other. I make every effort to treat my children with respect and expect the same of them. If we can't communicate something without breaking trust publicly, we wait and discuss it later. It shows respect in both directions. My children know I will be there for them. It models my value system and sets an expectation for them. Equally important, I know they will show up for me as well, in the age-appropriate capacity they are capable of showing up.

Children should experience small losses so they understand the world around them is not always in their favor. The world is not fair. However, children are not prepared for loss as meaningful, intense, and permanent as death.

Some children disconnect. They act like nothing has happened. That is not necessarily good. At some point, they will need to go deep and work those feeling through. Perhaps you will know they are moving through grief when they are acting out … difficult, rebellious, emotional … this could be the child's way of distancing themselves, creating a barrier between their own feelings and the world they find treacherous. If the child doesn't care about anyone or anything, this could be a protection from being hurt. If you don't love, you won't feel the pain of loss at this deep level again. It hurts too much to repeat. If they make a friend, they might lose the friend and they cannot bear to face that pain of loss again.

Time, love, support, patience are remedies to heal this. You can help create a safe space for them to experience the healing time, love, support, and patience. However, you also need time, love, support, and patience. In a life filled with expectations, it is challenging, and doable, to find them. You can choose your medium and pursue your path through work, meditation, downtime, writing, art, friends, family, fun, exercise, travel, adventure, self-care. You can guide the children in the same way.

We were not good at family game nights and sports. We did have engaging sit-down dinner conversations and we love going on adventures. We make an effort to spark dinner topics and I have combined adventures with healthy exercise by coordinating training for organized running events and traveling to experience them with the children. When they rebel, I do not match their emotional frustration. I hold space for them. When they have peeled back a proverbial onion layer of angst, I invite them to come up with another healthy, family-oriented solution to sharing time, love and support together. No one said it was going to be easy.

After losing their father, the children were concerned about being separated from me. Eventually, they loosened their grip and started sleeping on their own as I reassured them that I am here and security plans are in place. They moved to their own beds on their own accord as I adjusted their spaces to be inviting to them again. In our case, I put up a canopy and added stuffed toys and blankets. I told them they were welcome with me. Eventually, they were comfortable enough to find their own spaces safe enough again. My understanding from widows is that most allow the children to stay as long as they like and return whenever they need ... remember that mom needs a good night's sleep to get through the day, too. Nourishing yourself through a good night's sleep is key.

Children Addressing Grief

Letting go doesn't mean you forget about a loved one. By letting go of the hold grief has on you, you can realize that there is so much more for you to be happy about and there are many beautiful people around you that love and care about you, and you want to enjoy and express your gratitude for their presence because at one point they will need to also leave this world and you don't want to miss out on them.

Rachel said she isn't willing to move through grief because she is worried she will forget daddy if she let's go of grief. We talked about the difference between grief and memories that create who you are and strengthen who you will become. To ensure the children don't feel like they are losing too many memories of Sean, I put together a photo album for each child with images of them with Sean and other loved ones. The reality is they didn't remember most of those moments, reminding me that it is natural not to remember everything ... even if it was important, fun, or funny. Witnesses to our lives help us remember and review events from a different perspective. The images all demonstrate that we as a family are close, adventurous, supportive, playful, curious and silly. In addition to the silly pictures, a few moments stood out to me: A proud father smiling at his newborn child, a newborn child smiling back at her father, and a loving parent consoling his daughter in his arms when she was sad. Others include a father tying his son's tie and a memory of father and son walking away in the snow, hand-in-hand.

Teamwork, Yes; But What about the Stuff You Aren't Capable of Teaching Them

Get up, get them up. It's just another day, with all the expectations of all the other days before. All the expectations that would move the children in a positive trajectory that wouldn't have been questioned if their father had not died. So, you help get them dressed, fed, and back on their tracks. Remember you are preparing yourself to be on your best trajectory as well. Eventually, you'll guide everyone to their success trajectories. Eventually, something will give you cause to smile … or laugh and remind you the value of life again.

As you know, you can't be everything to everyone all the time, everywhere, everyone needs you. The solution is to surround yourself and your children with people who love them so they have a safe community everywhere they go, especially when you are not there with them.

What is the most important role you can fill for your children? In my case, it is comfort and guidance. Surround them with people who love them. They have lost control of so much, including their father. Give them control of something, routine: bedtime routine, and maybe an unconditionally loving pet? Give a little. It's impossible to think things will be the same, do what you can do, get done what you can get done. As my late husband said when the white table cloth, multi-course meals stopped, "The service levels have decreased." You can only do what you can do. That leaves a whole lot of gaps including high-level physics topics at the dinner table. In addition to learning to order things and food online which come to us, I've found drivers to help get the children around town and when they were ready, I taught them to use public transportation. Occasionally I call for backup. A neighbor who cooks with the children. A dance instructor who sees talent and provides an opportunity for a moment to shine. A stable owner who knows the value of trusting a heart-broken little girl with a super loving horse. Scouting troops who welcome the one-parent kid. It takes a village to raise a child. Find the right village for your children.

When They Need More Than You Have to Give and What It's Going to Take to Inspire Them Forward

Comfort tools are the tools you use to rebalance your energy. This list grows in the most fantastic way every time I conduct a workshop because people re-stabilize and re-energize in different ways. If you made a list of things that make you happy, this is a good time to call upon it. Otherwise, get that list started so you aren't starting on a blank page when emotions spiral.

Comfort tools are unique to each child. A cozy blanket, an experience or outing, time with Mom, a treasure like a pair of sunglasses a piece of jewelry passed down from generation to generation, something new that is just for them, a toy, a trinket, typically something intangible or something to hold on to that is real, that they can grasp. So much is out of reach or their control, something real is comforting in the real world. For my children, time and adventures with friends and animals, engineering things like Lego, Minecraft, and Transformers are comfort tools and new versions of these favorites are "currency." Currency is something the children find valuable enough they may step just outside their comfort zone to attain it. Through the years, I've reinvented ways to earn points that translate into what they value. Accomplishing developmentally age-appropriate tasks, small behavior changes are ways to earn points toward a coveted horse-riding lesson or a computer 3D modeling tool.

When I was a little girl … the children love stories that start this way. I am the youngest of four children. My siblings and I would sometimes spend the night outside in the backyard. We slept on shredding wicker lounge chairs that were reported to have once been owned by Roy Rogers, an American singer and cowboy actor. Perhaps his horse, Trigger, nibbled at the wicker or something because they were a bit prickly and they closed up on you if you didn't sit on them just right. But that would not have stopped my dad from purchasing them at a garage sale if someone said Roy Rogers owned them.

We children used to spend the night in the backyard on these chaise lounge chairs. We looked up at the stars and my siblings told me that one of the stars, named Charlie, would come down and land in our backyard. Charlie the Star would take us on a ride across the heavens. And there were free candy machines in the star. Candy and a ride across the heavens! What could be better than that? This was going to be great.

There was one catch: I had to stay awake until Charlie landed on the lawn. My siblings were not going to wake me up for a ride across the heavens if I fell asleep. They were not going to wake me up for free candy if I fell asleep. But I fell asleep every time. When Charlie the Star landed on our back-yard lawn, my siblings went for a ride across the heavens and ate candy from free candy machines while I slept on Roy Rogers' rickety old fold-up wicker furniture in our backyard. Maybe next time, I would be able to stay awake a little longer.

Some goals are too hard to achieve. I simply could not stay awake even for the promise of an incredible reward. When the children are spending too much time playing video games that were once their currency and then an addiction, it may be time to adjust the currency to invite them back into the real world. This is an ever-changing system. You know best where to set boundaries, discipline, and rewards.

Obligation Richter Scale

The "Obligation Richter Scale" is a tool to gauge value and assess the importance on something. If I would like the children to join me at an event, I note the importance of the event by applying a numeric value to it. If the event is rated a ten on the "Obligation Richter Scale," they must re-prioritize and participate. I'd love them to join me, but it is really up to them if it is rated a seven. With a rating of a five, it is a give or take whether they participate or not. For example, showing up to a family reunion was a ten. Attending a gathering of friends could be a six or a seven. Waiting for their sibling while they engaged in a peer's jumpy-house party is a much lower number. This tool has been handy for us to assess a value of importance on supporting each other at events.

As the Obligation Richter Scale demonstrates the responsibility and commitment to participate in activities together, I naturally use a similar scale to allocate resources. When I was young, I spent money on different things including candy, clothes, gas, and a car. Then the focus was on education and learning. It didn't take long to calculate dollars based on airline tickets to exotic places. It followed that I invested in baby gear and teeny, tiny outfits. I quickly understood the importance of Legos, stuffed animals, toys, and tiaras. Now I recognize the value of enriching the children to give them the knowledge and skills to become well-rounded, contributors, and leaders in the community. The children and I continue to use the Obligation Richter scale to get an idea of the importance we place on an event or behavior. It helps to apply a value to things.

Creating a Resilient Family

How can you honor your late husband? Knowing you've created a ceremony, tradition something meaningful to you and the children, you will free yourself to move forward knowing you've done what you can do.

Some families celebrate their late father's birthday by doing things he enjoyed, especially things he enjoyed doing with them. Sometimes, we visit the cemetery. We go to Sushi. We share "Remember that time when…." stories. We make waffles. We drive his car.

What's Important in Life Right Now

Returning to School

The children have had a significant role change and going back to school may be difficult with this new identity. As happy as they are for the other children having good experiences, or even bad ones, with their dad, it is natural for them to be envious they don't ever get to rely on him again. Schoolmates are not always diplomatic. "Ah, you are sad because your dog died and your dad died and you have to write a personal narrative about it. Oh, too bad." Doesn't make working in partnerships in English class any easier. You can give your children a one sentence script to respond to comments about dad's absence. "My father has passed away." And just stop there. Or they don't have to answer questions. Your child can refer any additional questions to the school counselor or Principal. It shouldn't take long for your children to wish to find "normal" again at school. They should feel that they can discuss what is on their mind. At the same time, they shouldn't have to talk about their loss publicly until they are ready. Sensitive topics are reserved for people on the inner circle. They are welcome to keep that conversation at home, where their thoughts can be honored appropriately. Surviving a return to the community is helpful with a reminder of the point people you and your children have chosen together in the event they need a moment for themselves. Put an appropriate game plan in place if your child feels they need to leave an environment like a classroom, how they should let the person in charge know they are taking a wellness moment and where they will be going, for example, to the school counselor's office.

Cell Phone

Every parent worries about their children. Sole parents may not have the back-up to rely on. As a result, sole parents have been known to provide a limited phone and plan for their children as early as eight or nine years old. There are apps on the phone that provide location information and provides the children with communication they may not make an effort for if they have to ask an adult to convey the message. This is a simple way to communicate in the event of emergencies or even a change in schedule. Overall the feedback I've received is that children in this situation have been relatively responsible with their phone usage. (We have had battery issues so we've purchased little back-up batteries they keep in their backpacks.) Some say children won't get a phone until they pay for it themselves teaching responsibility and accountability. Like on the computer there are apps to filter websites, view history, and provide rewards. You can share educational videos of different ways children can get into and avoid trouble online to make sure they really understand and it is not just them thinking their Mom is paranoid. Videos of people tracking children with what personal information they post to kidnap them, children going to juvenile detention for bullying, and children getting criminally charged for sharing inappropriate pictures of friends that could be considered child porn (Cleavage of a fourteen-year-old girl is illegal). We discussed at length about how the internet is forever and not all of it is good. With great responsibility comes great danger.

Parenting Tricks That Work Every Time

Not always perfect in my parenting, I have come up with a couple of tricks that the children and I find helpful and they help me keep my cool even if they are emotional.

Lead, Follow, or Get Out of the Way

Rachel was playing with some Lego yacht toy she had built. The adventure was outstanding as the imaginary friends were cruising the world and embracing cultures everywhere. Until one of the pieces were lost while the imaginary friends were docked in their imaginary port. The real problem was the meltdown Rachel had over the lost toy piece. At wits end, Sean suggested she take the lead of the story and figure something out, follow along with whatever story he was about to manifest, or get out of the way so the yacht could be repaired. I was surprised Rachel chose to follow. (It was probably the first and last time she has chosen to follow, but who wouldn't want to know what could happen next in the imaginary tale.) Sean continued the game and suggested the imaginary friends find a really cool Marine tech center where a super qualified boat fixer could repair the boat with the colors of that country. Then Rachel was proud of the mismatched piece in the toy yacht because it had a storyline.

Sometimes giving them a reasonable choice, or some control of something in an out-of-control situation provides stabilization and they can work through things more easily.

Listen, Guide, or Help

Now that the children are a little older, I can ask them would they like me to listen, give my opinion and guide, or get involved, help. I know they are going to do what they want when I am not there, so I thought at least this way they could solicit my input and know how I feel about things. I appreciate they consider my perspective and advice. The hard part is respecting which option they choose. If I feel I need to override and get involved, I do ask for their authorization or let them know why I am overriding their decision.

Rachel was an avid swimmer, but swim team didn't work for us. Her choice was to swim with a mermaid tail. It is a pretty impressive thing to see her swimming with this fabric covered fin. There is a lot of abdominal work involved. She is sure to get lots of wonderful attention when we travel with her mermaid tail. We were out on adventure when she realized she had outgrown her mermaid tail. She had made a friend and her question to me was a generous one. Should she gift the mermaid tail she had outgrown to this new friend who is smaller than she? I asked if I should listen, guide, or help. At first, Rachel asked me to just listen. So, I gave her my full attention. Then she realized she needed more, so she invited my opinion and authorization. I complimented her on her generous nature to gift something so valuable to someone who can continue to enjoy it when she no longer can. There was hesitation in her voice so I asked a few more questions. What would be the consequence of giving this new friend the tail? That girl would receive all the attention and awe Rachel had known while enjoying the tail. She would be happy for the girl but devastated not for the loss of the tail, but the loss of attention and concern the friend would play with the tail and not Rachel. The original decision was to gift the mermaid tail closer to the end of our adventure so they could enjoy their friendship without Rachel creating a situation that could take attention away from their playing together and the focus would be on the other girl with Rachel's too small mermaid tail. She seemed happy with that decision. As it turned out, we found a larger tail that fit Rachel and the friends could play Mermaids together.

Growing at the Speed of Children

Remember when the children were little? They grew wide and then they grew long, then they grew thick and then they grew tall? Well, growth through grief is no different (For you as well.) Realize there will be times when they feel they have got this, and other times they need you and their comfort tools more than ever. It is all part of the process, like a tree growing a thick, sturdy trunk before it grows any taller. The "thick" times are when they are stabilizing. Stick with them as they grow through grief, move through emotions and their identity changes to stand on their own bit by bit.

Quibbling Siblings

It is interesting to me to realize the children continue to play their older/younger sibling roles. Once I realized whatever they were doing that drove me to impatience was both age-appropriate and on a grand scale a 'level one' issue, I found listening to their challenges and competitions with each other as a form of entertainment rather than an annoyance. What I learned was they are establishing their independence and practicing negotiations with each other. The entertaining part was understanding that they were competing over meaningless interactions. When we are dealing with serious and real issues, we stand together. One of my favorite examples was when they were debating over a brush and staring at an empty open cupboard. They were arguing over a pretend remote control to determine what they should watch on the imaginary television in the empty cupboard. I suggested they each watch their own pretend show on the pretend television. Clearly, I had no idea what they were facing based on the way they looked at me. I let them work things like that out on their own more often than not.

Some things they need to figure out together. The real stuff they will seek your advice with. As the parent, this is another opportunity to offer: listen, guide, or help.

The Power of Listening

What is the question behind the question? So often the children make a statement and expect us to cycle through the seven possibilities we need to ensure they are brought back to homeostasis. As they become more mature, and their needs are more complex they are also more independent. It is important to remind them to ask for what they want. Often, they don't know what they want, but with a simple line of questioning a complaint can turn into something they have control over. It is empowering to be their guide rather than the problem solver. Plus, it takes so much burden off of you as they mature. What is the unanswered question they are asking when they say something like, I am cold. I ask, "Are you sharing your life experience with me? Are you complaining? Are you blaming someone for lowering the temperature in your environment? Are you expecting someone to read your mind and acknowledge you? Do you need to adjust something? Should you take control of your conditions and put on a sweater or find a warmer situation? There is not enough information in, I am cold." The children want control over things in their life. Listening to the meaning behind the message gives you insight into how you can give them control over something they can control. In addition to giving them some control, this reminds them they are responsible for their lives and it is not someone else's responsibility to make things perfect for them. Ultimately, they are learning to take responsibility for their lives.

How to Find Other Advocates

You will know who will best support the interest of your children.

The school Principal and teachers were supportive. In our case, they showed up. The children were invited to let teachers know they were going to the office to have alone time or seek the school counselor out if triggers created emotions that were too much for the classroom routines. They set codes so they didn't have to announce the vulnerability.

Their peers are great support. I welcomed the children to invite their closest friends to their father's funeral, memorial, and to stay over for a few nights. It is remarkable to see how their friends stayed nearby. They didn't have the right words to say to make anything better. The children somehow knew they didn't need words. So they didn't make things up like we grown-ups tend to do in an effort to make everything okay. The children's friends just stayed nearby. They hung out in the children's rooms. They coaxed them outside and attempted to play. Their friends kept their mind off the topic Their friends who "showed up" will continue to be their forever friends. These are peers who understand in a way no one else ever will.

It doesn't always work. When it doesn't, try a different way.

As compassionate and understanding as children are, there are other children with their own stories that may be as treacherous as the loss of a father which creates behaviors that are less than desirable. It is challenging to be partnered with the kid who beat you up on the flag football field and when instructed to write a personal narrative teases, "Oh, you are sad because your dog died and your dad died." It doesn't always create inspired writing. At times like these, it is more important to think big picture on the impact the short-term events have on the children. Rachel noted that there are three ways to respond to bullies: Do nothing and eventually they get bored and move on. You can retaliate, but that often results in the bully coming back with equal or greater force. You can try getting a grown-up and end up with the title of "snitch." Changing the environment is the other option.

We will always be envious of the fathers skipping and laughing with their children. We are happy for them and sad for our loss. Scouting creates natural opportunities for surrogate role models. It is also filled with parent-child pairs that always come first.

As painful as it may seem, the children found some comfort in meeting teens, young adults, and grown-ups who lost a parent when they were young. It helped them see how people can survive and thrive despite this challenge.

And most big impact stories have characters who have lost a parent or two, it helps us sympathize for them more. As difficult as it is to see it played out over and again, it is a reminder that we can survive with loss.

Mistakes – SWOT Analysis for Kids

We all make mistakes. The best way I've learned to get through them is to acknowledge them. "My bad." Own it. Your children will see that no one is perfect and it gives them greater opportunity to take risks. They will see you are doing the best you can if you acknowledge your intent, substantiate why you took the actions you did, recognize where things didn't go as anticipated and then note what you could have done better or things you can do to plan for a better outcome next time.

Naturally, the children will make mistakes, as well. Allow them the space to make them and collaborate in the same way you role model for them so they, too, can learn how to self-improve despite setbacks and failed attempts.

We do a SWOT analysis, acknowledging strengths, weaknesses, opportunities, and threats, when we are a standstill. I pull the stickies out and we post each child's strengths and superpower skills, we note their weaknesses and then evaluate opportunities that will drive them to the next level and bring them toward what they are looking to achieve. Threats are the last component to evaluate and discuss how to overcome obstacles that prevent their growth, as well as note consequences to not overcoming the obstacles. Here is a brief example:

Perhaps you guide your child this way – First you highlight your child's strengths, include having an analytical mind and being an innovator and inventor. Sometimes there is a weakness intrinsic to a strength. You can add that one example of this is an ability to do math in your head, not showing your work is preventing your teachers from assessing the thought process you are using to demonstrate you understand the concepts. Another more straightforward weakness is lack of confidence advocating for yourself and speaking with your teacher about this concern.

Then consider opportunities to overcome weaknesses like showing your work on paper so the teacher can follow your thought process and grade you respectfully. Perhaps work with the tutor to slow down the process enough to allow others to be certain you understand the mathematical process

It is important to evaluate the consequences. In some cases, the worst-case scenario is not a big deal. In others, failure is not an option and you have to keep trying a different approach until you get what you need. In this example, if you don't show your work, you are not getting credited for it. Therefore, your teachers are not giving you the grades you wish to move forward in your academics. You could flunk or be held back.

Big and Fine Motor Skills and Intellectual Pursuits

We balanced our activities out to ensure we engaged in big motor skill activities like skiing, running, rock-climbing, dancing, hiking, walking the dog (a lot), fine motor skills including playing with Lego, doing artwork, drawing, playing cello and violin and massaging mommy's feet while she reads or makes up fantastic stories (Oh did I confess that?) with additional activities to stimulate intellectual curiosity like playing strategic games (We enjoyed developing scavenger hunts for the children with increasingly encoded clues for them to follow.) We teach the children to cook … we all benefit from that. We should teach them to be more fastidious, but all in good time. To us, it was more important we ate well than we did the dishes right away. We also enjoyed community time and we would teach the children things like the three-corner compliment, the three-point thank you, and the four-step apology (detailed later) providing structure to important social interactions and the children enjoyed seeing the consequences of their behaviors with people.

CHAPTER 8:

Career, Resource, and Revenue

Curiosity and the pursuit of interesting passions provides depth and interest to life. Is the intersection of your purpose/passion and skill set providing you with the revenue you need to support your future life?

Revenue and resources are the leverage and means by which you attain what you would like and need. You may need to call upon your resources, your Advisory Board, to update your resume and refocus your career. Realize that in the process you are adjusting your identity as your professional and personal needs and goals change.

What Happens When You Are Functionally Catatonic

There was a time when staring into space was really the only option I could come up with. It's not in line with my personality, but I was meditating and resting, allowing the nothing in, hoping the clouds would open and the sun would light a clear path. Nothing. I got up and went through the motions. I did what was required of me, nothing more. Outsiders may not have even noticed that I had reeled in my energy, winding it so tight like a cocoon, protecting me from every external stimulus that was not the absolute minimum requirement. It takes internal inertia to transition from holding on to moving on. It literally took my Advisory Board members to shake me out of it. Good thing I had put them in place. To this day, I'm not sure how I would have navigated through that metamorphosis on my own.

It took Carol a year after her late husband passed to feel really alive again. It is not easy for anyone to reach out to make new friends. She said on day 365, she woke up and had new energy with which she used to reach out to establish social opportunities. For her, it was building relationships in her religious community and creating deep friendships playing Mah Jong. She wanted to be a competent Mah Jong player, so she set up the game in her living room and played all four players' hands until she knew she understood the game well enough to be an engaging opponent. When she won too many rounds, she received scowls from her new friends. She learned to throw her game a bit until she knew how hard to play in her new social circle. When a friend who she became particularly close with moved, she had to expand her Relationship Spiral to include more people with whom she could find things in common. I remember watching her navigate her path by taking care of her physical health, going to the gym, getting a spray tan, getting her hair done, dressing up and spending time with the family more than going through the motions. That is what it took, enough courage and desire to do something even though it was hard, and do it anyway.

Widowhood is not a choice. It is your choice to decide how you would like to identify yourself and lay out the stepping stones to fulfill your role.

There is no word in the English language that represents when a loved one is comforting you for their impending loss. Fell in love, married, had children. That is three different personal identity changes. I've worked in the financial, medical, health and fitness, academic, advertising and marketing, industries ... all of them identity changes. Once I understood how business processes work, it was a transferable skill.

Then my husband became ill and died. That left me with a new identity: widow and sole-parent.

Here I am in a role no one is eager to take on, few understand and even fewer have a set of steps to navigate with any grace or ease. So, I wrote this book to share some things I've learned in the hope you can benefit from my experience.

Life is a gift. You've been given the gift. It is up to you to determine how you choose to enjoy the gift.

Who Am I Now?

I had changed industries several times in my professional life, recreating myself in new roles. This was actually helpful in my ability to change my role in my personal life. From accelerated growth in the financial industry, world-wide train the trainer opportunities in the fitness industry, directing the strategic partnerships, sales and service departments in the publishing arena and refining health care quality as a social scientist in the Department of Medicine for Stanford, I have enjoyed many professional roles all coinciding at the intersection of sharing my skills, expertise, passions and life experience to widows who are sole parents with the tools to navigate your way toward a full and happy life for you and your children. I couldn't have anticipated this role, but I do get to fill my goal of creating a legacy by helping others find their success through it.

Who Should You Be? – Passion/Purpose/Income

Chart the things you love to do and figure out the intersections between your talent and your passions. Then evaluate what of those things you can earn an income doing. Look at job descriptions and select what is most appealing to you about them. Put those highlights all together and see if you can create your dream job description. With that, you've got resume topics to highlight in your experience and roles for which you can apply with confidence.

Smell of Desperation

It was a day where I let things bother me. There were a couple of gorgeous grad students in their workout clothes, straight blonde hair and eyelashes, buying expensive cups of coffee talking about some old waste of a human with whom they are being forced to be in a study group. According to them, he graduated college without a clue as to what do with his life, didn't make anything of himself and then returned to grad school, at Stanford, and now they are being forced to study with this thirty-year-old without a future.

One of the girls went on to discuss how she and her mom were flying somewhere to go clothes shopping next week. I thought to myself, "I hope your support group doesn't know how you feel about them."

Soon thereafter, I had set up a call with a career counselor to help me update my resume. The first half of the call went as I imagined it would. I wrote down the adjectives the counselor used to describe me including bright, innovative, articulate, problem-solver, etc. Then she asked why I'm looking for a job at this time. Am I just starting my search? No, I was looking a little over a year ago when my husband got cancer … and I gave her the high-level overview of our difficult situation. I realize I have been struggling through this hard time for over a year and she is just hearing about it. Her tune changed to, "Oh, you absolutely must be seeing a therapist. And people should be helping you, taking the children overnight and bringing you meals." Now, I realize she is trying to help, so I pointed out that I am asking for specific help … from her to help me with my resume. I asked if I could please separate my personal from my professional life. She said no because my network knows what is going on with me … and that I smell of desperation.

Later, I took Rachel to her therapist who analyzed me after I told her a story and laughed. "Ah, I see you use humor as a form of stress relief." And she wrote down a few notes. At least I use humor as stress relief.

Then I took Rachel to ballet where she was sitting on my lap enjoying hanging on me. She commented, "I hope I never get a wrinkly neck." I hope one day you do as it means you've aged nicely. "Yeah, well, people with wrinkly necks don't run very fast." The other mommy's nearby sunk a bit knowing they are also slow running and wrinkly necked. I kissed Rachel and sent her on her way with the other perfectly formed ponies dressed in white leotards dancing to Sleeping Beauty.

At dinner that evening, Rachel asked how my day was. I reflected saying I took some hits today that typically I would let slide, but they added up, including someone said I smelled of desperation. Rachel jumped off her chair to take a long whiff of me and responded, "You don't smell of desperation, mommy. You smell of rosemary … and old lady."

I asked if I could please be excused. Of course, none of them meant harm. Pursue your own passion and don't let anyone or anything deter you.

Don't Sign for the Gifts You Don't Want

There are some gifts you can refuse to accept. If the UPS delivers a package that you did not order, you don't accept the package. I did not need to accept or even authorize the messages being sent to me on that day. Sure it might be an extra challenge to let go of the "hits" people send. Increase your resilience, and be the person you would like to become.

You Are Too Important to Waste Your Time on That

Time can neither be saved nor stored; it can only be used more effectively. I have learned we can prioritize our activities and delegate some, but the ones we take on are the ones that carve our character and it is what we do with the time we have that writes the stories of our lives.

In college, I did a research project on time management. Time had been invented back then. Some of my major discoveries included a variety of approaches people take to accomplish tasks. I found it interesting that some people take on a project whereas others take on the time constraint. Each approach has a unique way to prioritize activities. One is more structured, the other allows for a more creative stance to get the same things done.

The Pareto principle, also known as the 80–20 rule, states that, for many events, roughly 80 percent of the effects come from 20 percent of the causes. Vilfredo Pareto, an Italian economist observed in 1906 that 80 percent of the land in Italy was owned by 20 percent of the population; Pareto developed the principle by observing that 20 percent of the pea pods in his garden contained 80 percent of the peas.

On a scale of zero to ten, how are you feeling eighty percent of the time? Can you achieve a moment at an "eight" this week? That would be music to my ears! Eventually, you will feel closer to your optimal zone more than 20 percent of the time. As you work toward your goals, you will feel higher on the scale 80 to 100 percent of the time. It takes work. Work works wonders.

Every day we use our ability to manage projects, priorities, and deadlines. What is your next big project?

What about timing? There is also a time to address things. What would it cost you to take a little extra time to stabilize your family emotionally? Assess your situation to determine how much time, money, and energy you have for downtime. If you make one big change, how does that affect other things? For example, getting a full-time job may mean you need to address who is caring for the children. That should not be an obstacle, simply a consideration.

Keep the Good Stuff

There are times in your life when there are things you simply cannot delegate. As a student, your work belongs to you and there is little that can be completed by others if you expect to be acknowledged for it. In business, there are teams of people who are specialists hired for a common goal, the mission, and vision of the business. It is possible to translate that to the mission and vision of your personal life and your children, then enlist specialists to contribute in their areas of expertise to achieve your goal. Keep the important things like life celebrations and routines that bring you closer with your children. If your best conversations happen while walking the dog, make time for that. Delegate the stuff that keeps you from doing your important work. For example, sharing or hiring someone to help transport children, do the housework or make a meal might provide you with the time and focus you need for career improvement or self-care.

You've Got to Start Somewhere – Secure Revenue and Resources

It is vital to stabilize things. At this point, if you haven't gone through the logistics checklist, go back and make sure you've got things in place to settle your late husband's "estate." The next step is to secure yourself and the children.

People behave differently when they are feeling secure. Confidence is built in when there is a safety net and they can take greater risks.

Stabilizing Forces

Food, clothing, shelter, relationships. Find the pockets of assets, revenue streams and ensure they outweigh the expenses. Easy to say. Challenging to do. Beyond a standard revenue stream from a job, look in places like:

- Programs established through your employer
- Project, part-time, temporary, consulting opportunities
- Investments
- Insurance
- Social Security
- Family and friend support
- Community and social organizations
- Unemployment, Disability, WIC, Food stamps

It is important to understand your financial position so you can see where you are now and what you need to adjust to plan for your and the children's future. Evaluate your fixed expenses, they happen every month like rent, and variable expenses you could skip like eating at restaurants.

Being organized is a challenge, but it makes your life a whole lot easier.

What if you need a job? Organizations are more open to onboarding women back into the workplace even after a gap in employment. Here are some quick steps to increase confidence and skill set to get back in the workforce.

Going back to work after a pause is a time of transition and can be a time when we are trying to discern our skills and the vision for ourselves and for our future. It is a time for renewal, and this process can help you assess your strengths, where you will be of value in the workforce and your direction.

Realize Your Superpowers

We all have internal skills within us to create our customized vision of who we are and who we wish to be. If one of your superpower skills is organizing, perhaps when you are feeling your strength is when you are utilizing your superpowers. Consider how you utilize your superpowers. Are your superpowers logistics, organization, intuition, problem-solving, conveying high-level concepts in an easy-to-understand way? Describe a time when you were proud of your accomplishment.

Stretch your strengths and strengthen your weaknesses. What are your weaknesses? Are you better working independently or in groups? How do you compensate for the things you are not strong at accomplishing? Your Advisory Board may be a good resource here. Evaluate options to counteract your weaknesses. We all have them, simply prepare for them and you are set. Reframe the situation to see all sides. Come from a point of compassion.

Evaluate when you are glowing with enthusiasm for whatever it is you enjoy doing. Some superpower skills identified include: integrity, intelligence, intuition, inspiration, energy/enthusiasm, playful spirit, truth/honesty, knowing what people need to solve their issues, knowing what makes people tick, instantly understand the core of a person, business management, and cohesiveness.

Allow your inner voice to guide you to solutions to strengthen your weaknesses. Would we say out loud to others what we say to ourselves internally? What happens when you adjust your mindset to "Would I want this for my dear child?" It would be unselfish if you represented someone you care about. To be available to anyone else, we need to love ourselves.

Because we are often better at advocating for others than ourselves, when negotiating, realize you are negotiating not only on your own behalf and your worth, but the value of your energies will bring enough revenue to support and sustain your children and their future.

Create your target vision by connecting with your future self to help determine which way you should direct your path. Align your superpowers with your target vision to determine your career trajectory.

Acknowledge Guides and Landmarks, access your Advisory Board, create specific, strategic, meaningful, measurable, achievable, relevant, and timely stepping stone goals to move toward your target vision.

Consider another iteration of your identity when selecting where you will apply to share your time in exchange for revenue and stability to move yourself and your children forward. What role is appropriate for you? Consider similar titles, which may have varying salary ranges attached to them. For example, an administrative assistant may be equally qualified for roles including, office administrator, office coordinator, administrative coordinator, office manager, and office assistant.

Which type of organization would you be proud to represent? What responsibilities would you feel competent to maintain? More than half of candidates say they accept a job because they like the corporate culture. Speak with current employees to determine if the culture and environment are a fit for you. That will help you figure out why it is great to work for an organization and decide if that brings you closer to your stepping stone or long-term vision goals. Align your superpowers and values with the role and how that position supports the business objectives. Identify how your experience and qualifications transfer to that role. You can note the general responsibilities and demonstrate how you have done similar things in the past and highlight the benefits and outcomes your effort made. Implement a strategy to make it easy for the prospective employer to see how you fit in the role they are trying to fill in their organization.

If you find the process of identifying your qualifications difficult, consider reaching out to me for guidance. Recognize what you have or need to attain to be an appropriate fit for an opportunity:

- Education, experience, and technical skills necessary.
- Job-specific hard skills: Formal education and training programs, apprenticeships, short-term training classes, online courses, certification programs, and on-the-job training.
- Transferrable skills: Communication, organization, presentation, teamwork, planning, and time management.
- Look at the corporate culture where you will feel comfortable, the salary range you need and any special requirements you may need to endure to accomplish the job. Extraordinary conditions applicable to the job (i.e., heavy lifting, exposure to temperature extremes, prolonged standing, or travel). Do they fit in your current lifestyle?

- Craft a Superpower Statement to include in your cover letter or attention-grabbing headline to help you stand out from the other applicants.
- Note two to four assets which make you an excellent fit for the job.
- For example, if you are applying for a public-facing role in finance, you may consider something like, "My strong mathematics skills, customer service orientation, attentiveness to detail and ability to work with precision make this job an excellent fit for me." Give examples of how and where you applied those skills.
- Review Job Posting
  - Compatibility
  - Does the role match your target vision
- Resume and Cover Letter
  - Match skills and qualifications to job requirements
  - Be prepared for objections
  - Track progress
- Show Up
  - Prepared
  - Well-informed
  - Professional – Ask questions and answer concerns before they are asked
- Follow-through
  - Ask your network to connect you
  - Informational and formal interviews
- Expand Network
  - Connect with other channels
  - Create touchpoints: follow-up with thank you notes and phone messages
- Tools for Renewal

- ○ Continue process
- ○ Balance effort with renewal

Track your progress by noting your action taken. You can keep a list of updates by company, job title, location, salary you noted, the salary range for that type of role in that city, the job requirements, keep a link to the post for quick reference so you have all the information you need available when you get a call. Keep records of the connections you have made with the organization, with whom, and the action that occurred. This will help you speak confidently when you do have the opportunity to shine for the hiring managers and influencers at the company.

You can develop a networking plan by reaching out to prior colleagues to help make referrals for you and act as a reference. Inform family and friends exactly what you are looking for in a job so they can be on the lookout. Update your social profiles and networks to note you are open for opportunities. Speaking with a recruiter is a great way to get an idea of what is going on in your industry at the current time and may have recommendations for you.

With your networking plan in place, you can reach out to set up appointments to make connections beyond your current scope. Ask people in a company of interest or someone in a similar role for an informational interview. Remember to get an insight into the company and the position so you have a clear understanding of the role you would fill in the position and how you could benefit the company in the current market. The next valuable thing you can do is ask for the next connection with someone in the company to continue to expand your reach in the industry of interest. Ask them about themselves.

Of course, track your progress noting status, your plan, the action taken, the result and the follow-up. I know a few people who were hired because of their organizational job search skills.

When you are asking the right questions to the right people, you should get what you are after. Even if what you learn is that you need to adjust course.

- For example, do you know anyone who knows someone who works in the arts? I am interested in working in the arts. I have a friend in a museum.
- I'm looking for information to see where my skill set fits. Who in the organization might I be able to talk to about that?
- Someone you know may introduce you to someone who may have insight into a skill set or organization because "I'm interested in X about what you are doing. Do you have ten minutes?" Respect the ten minutes and ask who else you can contact about this subject.

Thank each person along the way. Cc: the others and leave the breadcrumbs.

Stabilizing your finances is a good way to increase your confidence. Grounding your relationships is another great way to move in the direction of becoming who you would like to be.

CHAPTER 9:

Recalibrating Relationships

It challenges us when we have trouble getting back on an even keel after a loss. My rose-colored glasses, with denial as the tint, provided me with a short reprieve until they were yanked off when I would find the children needed me because they were not ready for the day-to-day ... or I wasn't. Just when I thought I was up and ready to start a project my energy waned. We all get frustrated when we aren't able to finish the projects we have on our "to-do" lists. I accomplished my top priority, walking the dog, and left it at that. I share a coffee with my mom grateful for the time to share together.

Beverly Clark said, "We need a witness to our lives. There are a billion people on the planet... I mean, what does anyone's life really mean? But in a marriage, you're promising to care about everything. The good things, the bad things, the terrible things, the mundane things... all of it, all of the time, every day. You're saying, 'Your life will not go unnoticed because I will notice it. Your life will not go un-witnessed because I will be your witness.'"

Oprah said, "Every single person you will ever meet shares that common desire. They want to know: 'Do you see me? Do you hear me? Does what I say mean anything to you?' Validate them. 'I see you. I hear you. And what you say matters.'"

We invite witnesses into our lives on an intimate basis when we build relationships, share conversations and life experiences. To witness the big events of our lives, we write announcement letters and invitations to honor rites of passage: birth, accomplishments, graduations, welcome into the family as in marriage and new children, and testament for loss.

Our pets act as spectators, never revealing an awkward moment, always sharing company with cheerful happiness every time we re-enter the room. We are witnesses and guides to the children as they learn and grow.

Our grand plan was to be present with the children while they were small, establishing stability and a strong sense of family. Once they were in school full days, I intended to return to work and recoup our resources used to witness the early years of the children.

It was impossible to anticipate these changing and trying times. I say, "We cannot stop the river; we can only change its course." Currently I feel I can only follow the flow of the path that is laid before me and be present on the journey, witnessing it together.

It is a humbling journey. Thank you for your support as you save us and our dignity during challenging times.

This journey feels less lonely with you along. It makes me realize that so often in our lives we perceive ourselves through the reflection of others. We have witnesses to our lives with shared experiences to "see us, hear us, and validate that we matter."

No one really knows "the right thing to say." So, forget searching for the right thing and know that we are grateful for your presence to witness this journey with us.

They Are Not in the Club

Other people have other priorities that intersect yours. That is good. You connect *somewhere*. You don't even want them to know what you are really going through and they really cannot understand if they haven't had the experience. They are not in the widows' club. Realize they are trying to connect in a way they can. They mean well. They want you to be happy. Forgive them for asking questions in a way that doesn't make sense based on your heal and rebuild timeline.

They seem to want to check a box off their list of concerns so they can move on to the next one. See if you can find a way to understand the meaning behind the message to find the goodness they are attempting to express.

How are you going to make it? (And they actually expect a realistic answer.) Followed by, judgments like, I don't know who you think you are doing whatever it is you are doing because that is not how a widow should behave. Back to the description, I would like to break down the misconception that widows should never experience joy of any kind. All that is other people's issues. Let it go and welcome the sun in whenever it shines.

Aren't you over that, yet?

Why aren't you working?

Why aren't the children winning American Idol competitions, being awarded Nobel prizes?

Some people cannot see, hear, or speak with me because I represent my late husband and it opens a wound too deep for them to re-experience. For some, it forces them to face their own mortality, and that is a topic that is best ignored.

Others follow me around. One of these stalkers could articulate that I am the closest thing to my late husband that remains, so he is sticking near me to maintain the relationship he had with my late husband.

One friend told me I may no longer hang out with married people and that those people are not my friends anymore because I am single now. That just hurt. It took me a bit to realize she was expressing insecurities in her marriage. As I thought she and I actually were friends, I said I've always respected her marriage to her husband and I have never and would never be a threat to that. I did the positive opposite and let her know that, as her friend, I am here for her. She later explained that two of her husband's friends left their partners for each other and she is worried he will do the same. It was not a reflection on me. She hasn't spoken with me since.

After a year of being compassionate, people just want you to be okay. They aren't quite as available to help out anymore. They've helped enough and expect you will be ready to be on your own two feet with everything figured out by now. Compassion fatigue sets in when what would benefit you is staggered love. And then there is this thing that happens that people stop handling you with kid gloves and it's like, "Hey, don't you know I'm sensitive and weak and hurting and my husband is dead? Why can't you help me? My husband died." And then you realize time healed their wounds even though you're still grieving. It may be time to evaluate where on your Relationship Spiral are people now.

I probably somehow set myself up for this. I often feel as if others see my life as a television series and they cannot wait to learn what happens during the next episode, the cliff-hanger, the season finale, the next season, etc. But people have the benefit of binge-watching shows these days and I don't (even want to) have the luxury of knowing what is going to happen next. Some people lean in and support in their way. Others disappear. There has been a shift in my social circle as a result of the loss of my late husband.

Difficult Conversations

Some people have compassion and understanding, others do not. Forgive them. It may be they cannot face mortality and this loss may remind them of their own. It may be out of sight, out of mind. I have a dear one who looked me in the eye with amazement, "Oh you are still alive!" Was she realizing I would not be buried with my husband like in the Egyptian era? Yes. Death and loss are difficult to comprehend. Do not expect more of them. Put them in the correct category in your Inspirational Advisory Board or further out on your Relationship Spiral. This is another area, like figuring out people's skill set to welcome their help, where it is up to you to put a plan in place and lead the conversation.

Where is everyone? It is not contagious. Everyone is facing mortality, representing our worst fear. Some are just looking at it with a sideways glance. There was a line outside the door at the memorial, but few who check in throughout the year. Did we support others who were going through this? I admit I wasn't as helpful and didn't know to follow up down the road. If there is any lesson learned for me, it's that I've become a better friend to those starting this journey. It's been years and I'm now able to reach out to others to help. I have also started reaching out to friends I haven't heard from in a while. Turns out, they had troubles going on but they didn't want to burden me. At the same time, I would like to be there for them as they have for us. It is part of being in a two-way relationship.

There Is More to Life Than Simply Being the One Who Didn't Die

Set the stage and set boundaries for people.

Early on, one of my friends who I talked with most days felt as if she couldn't call me anymore, or interrupt me, or share her own woes because they didn't compare. She certainly didn't want to brag about any of life's wins. That left me alone, disconnected from someone else I shared my life with on most days. I couldn't let that happen. That would have been another loss. So, I set the expectations. We will continue to talk about everything, good, bad, brag even though we were experiencing very different times in our lives it was important we shared our lives with each other. And yes, sometimes it hurts to hear the loving father tales or the big decisions made over luxuries. However, our deep friendship was more important than the different phases in our lives and I wasn't planning on staying on the bottom forever. It was a reminder that there is more to life than simply being the one who didn't die.

Tell them it is okay to share their stories, good, bad whatever. Give them permission to speak of your lost love. Or, ask if it is okay to speak of him. Not that you should have to, but it sets the tone and removes the concern.

It is a personal decision to acknowledge where your late husband "lives" in your daily conversation. What I've seen is that over time he remains closer to the heart and not so much on the surface of conversations.

When people say things that do not resonate with you, take a breath and ask yourself what is the meaning behind the message. Don't compare your situation to theirs, they probably cannot understand the impact of the loss of your loved one and that is a good thing. Often, they are sharing themselves with you, it doesn't always come out smoothly. Realize they are sharing their story and welcome they are opening up to you about what they are experiencing and going through. That is a good thing. When you are having a great day, you will want them to revel in it with you.

Role Changes

Ours was a relationship of communication, respect, and trust. We made decisions based on what would be in the best interest of our entire family, not just us as individuals.

Utilizing the Relationship Spiral to ensure you are surrounded by the right people, it may be time to recalibrate relationships. Relationships change since your husband passed. As well, it is relevant to free some people up while welcoming others in, based on where they fit in your life. Some people will come closer in as they will be more aligned with you in your life as it is now.

You've been dealt a challenging hand…a powerful hand.

You've experienced a full range of life emotions.

Trust people. Some will betray that trust. That hurts. It doesn't mean you should not trust again. There are trustworthy people. The only way to know if someone can keep a secret is to share one and know it was secure. Then, bigger trust can be earned.

Trust yourself that you can do this.

Who Can Be Your Everything

The more I loved my husband, the more I needed my girlfriends is something I used to say … when I had my husband. I realized this one day as we were driving along and I wanted to share something with him … about the way I was feeling about him … that was so fantastic. It is a bit awkward to tell someone how amazing they are and how wonderful they make you feel and so on and so forth. Really, it is lovely to provide this feedback to someone, if they are at an appropriate point in the relationship to hear it and relish it. So, I shared it with him. He appreciated hearing the positive way he made me feel. He shared some lovely things with me, and things grew from there.

However, I needed something more. I wanted to keep reliving the moment by talking about it again … and again. He did not need that. So, I asked if he would act as one of my girlfriends so I could share the story again. He obliged. He responded in some sweet, sassy, girlfriend-y way.

For some reason, I really wanted to relive it by sharing it again. I realized quickly, that he did not need to hear this story again, so I waited to tell a summarized version to a friend and that was fine. When my next friend asked, "How are you?" I was eager to share my story again … and again.

I loved reliving the story by retelling it. However, my late husband experienced the story and heard it twice. It was a happy thing of the past for him. At that moment, I realized he could not be everything I needed. Because I need to relive the moment by sharing the story beyond his capacity to continue listening to it.

He learned that the way he would propose marriage to me would go down in history to be repeated throughout the years, so he better make it good. He did create a perfect on-bended-knee request … after I made it clear the trial proposal would not be the one I wished to share with our children.

The lesson is that one person cannot be your everything. As much as they try, they may not be able to provide you with 100 percent of your daily recommended requirement of everything at every moment, every time. Parents try to provide for their children. Partners try to offer for their partners. If the system breaks down and we rely too heavily on someone, often times it results in outward blame as if they caused our dissatisfaction. That is inappropriately placed responsibility put on someone else.

That leads you to the reality that we are responsible for our own happiness. It is your responsibility to care for your personal health and well-being. It is your choice to make the right decision on your own behalf, not someone else's. Occasionally, there is the gift of someone providing you with what you need or desire. That is a true gift and should be appreciated.

It is vitally important that we realize we are complex creatures and to create a scenario in which we receive all the things a complex creature needs, physically, emotionally, spiritually in relationships, we are filling an intricate puzzle. So when I say, "The more I loved my husband, the more I needed my girlfriends," I mean that my late husband filled a very wonderful space in my life. He provided me with confidence, support, unconditional love … the guy knew me, really knew me and still, he liked and loved me…. He was a wonderful partner in every way, including in parenting. It was inappropriate of me to ask him to hear my same story a thousand times. He was the wrong puzzle piece for that. He was not the right person to go to for some things because they were not his expertise. It took tremendous pressure off of our relationship when I realized his (tremendous) capacity and his limits.

There are people who are great as teammates. There are those that enjoy discussing a movie, going dancing, sitting around, fixing up houses, start a business, do the finances, bounce ideas off of, whatever it may be. It is really too much to expect one person to do it all. So fill your life with a variety of important people who complete your complex puzzle needs, which change over time.

The Missing Piece

As a widow, I've lost my husband. With that loss went my partner, my pillow talk, the person who cherishes and values me, one soul I can rely on no matter what, one who knows me so well and still likes me. I was fat and happy. I have lost my clear path and partner in my future. The children's parent, guide, embrace, reassurance, the person who wouldn't let our daughter leave the house with those clothes on, the guy who played with our son, the emergency contact, someone to "hold this," help me with this. The guy to fix the computer and ensure we don't get hacked not only technologically, but in life.

Shel Silverstein wrote a story about the missing piece.

As a widow, I feel like a jigsaw puzzle with a piece missing. I understand when someone loses a limb there is phantom pain. Going through the process of figuring out activities of daily living without a limb and perhaps with a prosthetic is a big life change. Figuring out life without my late husband is a big life-change, as well. Not my literal heart, but my proverbial heart has been shattered and no one can see that I am missing a big piece of myself, my identity, my partnership, my co-parent, my bed-warmer, my other half, my future as I had it planned, my old-age plan. I find people are disappointed in me. Disappointed that I am not doing more than before to compensate for his loss. I am not enough to provide quality time, embraces, inspiration, and support through grief, puberty, and homework for each of the children, all while grief bangs my head against the wall, throws me to the floor, and steps on my neck when I am trying to get something done. I need a prosthetic husband. I could use the assist, the visual representation indicating that something is missing. Where is staggered love? I am lonely. My true friends and well-wishers offer what they can, but it is just me here left to be strong and courageous, determine our future, to be able to provide two incomes, make all the important decisions and to figure out what happens after the happily ever after.

In Shel Silverstein's story in search of the missing piece, it goes on about the adventures of its sing-song life trying on "relationships" until, at last, it finds a piece that acknowledges it can be someone's fulfilling piece and still be its own piece. Eventually, the missing piece is left as its own piece and the adventures continue. In this case, the reminder is that even if you found a soul mate. You can have more than one soul mate.

My sweet daughter Rachel helped me realize that even though I myself as the jigsaw piece felt complete with my late husband, I have changed since losing him. As a result, I need a different shaped piece to continue my future adventures.

And when it all comes down to it, I've learned that what I need is to trust myself and build an Inspirational Advisory Board so I have Subject Matter Experts to add input into my decisions.

The lessons I've learned help me trust myself and my decisions. I am confident and my inner voice is kind. I prioritize what is actually really important. I advocate for myself and my children even if that means I am not going along with accepted societal norms. I align my values with the skills and experience I have to share with the world with my everyday intentions focused to positively impact those I can help the most. Each day I continue to become the person I strive to be with the intention of leaving a brilliant legacy in my wake. It is enriching to fill your life with connections, people, who hold different roles along your Relationship Spiral while on your life journey. Whether you share a moment or a lifetime together, you can learn from one another. When you understand you are enough and can do this on your own, and you are not confusing longing for connection with longing for love, you may be open to inviting someone to be a partner.

You have changed since you were with your late husband, here are some steps to consider when you are ready to invite in a new partner:

Take What You Need and Leave the Rest Behind

I will share the same advice I give to new parents. Listen to everything people have to say with an open mind because you might learn a thing or two. They are sharing their truth with you. There may be pearls of wisdom in there that you value. They are telling you who they are, and who they are to you as they speak their thoughts, opinions, and ideas. Thank them for their insight and sharing their experience with you. Take what you need and then do whatever is right for your family. Otherwise you are trying to please others who don't have the whole story. They mean well, but this is your life and your family to make decisions for.

I fall into the trap of trying to please everyone. It is impossible. A dear one gave me some great advice when she saw me falling apart as I was unable to please everyone and ended up pleasing no one. Most importantly I was being crushed by the effort which resulted in me not being able to take care of myself or my children. Here are her valuable words, "Where are your Wonder Woman cuffs and shield? Use those wrist cuffs to deflect what doesn't serve you. Let other people's opinions go, and do what is right for you." Of course, that philosophy doesn't apply to her, I should do what she says. She did purchase two sparkly bracelets for me to wear as a reminder to go out in the world on my own mission, not other's.

Widowhood Status

A status we don't wish on anyone. Do not join this club. The initiation is too dear. We had already lost earning revenue, our housing, and our community.

The first time I realized that my late husband getting cancer and dying would cause me to change my status was one of many role-changing, earth-shattering, alarming, disturbing, off-putting realities I was forced to face. I was out with friends. There was an unmarried, available male in the group. He extended the invitation to set up time with me if I'd like to talk. It was a generous, authentic offer with presumably nothing behind it. The guy is innocent. At that moment, however, a gameshow curtain was lifted with the loud announcer exclaiming I had just won "*A New Place in Your Social Life!*" Come on down. I am the next contestant in the game of "Being Single." I was awarded the undesirable and unwanted title of Widow, with two children. I loved the roles of girlfriend, fiancée, wife, and mother. In my mind, "Widow" is the auntie who has to be invited to the event, wears loud lipstick but you have to kiss her anyway even if she smells of ancient bathroom products, and she always ends up crying in the back corner of the room. Or worse, "Widow" could be the snarly lady down in the unkempt house at the end of the street, so skip that house when trick-or-treating because she is scary. Furthermore, when someone finds out I didn't win what was behind door number two in the proverbial game show of life, and now I am a widow, it is a total conversation buzz kill with apologies abounding. Ugh!

I should apologize to the fellow who offered to talk. It was me, not him.

Now I am this new thing – Widow. Once Sean passed, I was encouraged to remove my wedding ring. Oh, this was a difficult act. When I was a little girl with the annual wish upon the birthday cake, I didn't wish for a pony. I imagined being with a loving husband and children. I wanted to grow up and be part of a loving family. The only thing I could think to do at the time was model myself after Samantha Stevens in the television series Bewitched and learn to cook, entertain, and major in Business, Marketing/Advertising. You can imagine how happy it made me to hear Sean's comment, "You just wave your hands over the flour and sugar canisters and magically out comes dinner." My little-girl birthday wishes had come true! Now I needed to remind myself the magic was not in the ring itself. But it fit so nicely and it was a symbol of such a lovely message, and I feel so lost and naked without it. I totally understand the draw of J.R. Tolkien's "Precious" ring in The Hobbit. Still, I see my ring hanging on a chain intermingled with Sean's ring and it calls to me to put it back on as if it could bring back Sean and make everything right again.

Now with my new title and no ring, I have entered a status I endeavored to shake: single. I updated my social media … and cried. I would have been blissfully happy sharing my old age with my late husband. We would have raised the children and kissed them goodbye as we sent them off to college. We would have danced around the living room as empty nesters and missed them terribly until they returned home with their dirty laundry and uncertainties of the future. We would have complained about our aches and pains and helped each other up and down stairs and so on and so forth. That is how it went, I suppose, just in fast forward from the cancer diagnosis from thirty-nine to forty-three years old for Sean instead of so much later. I will walk the path my late husband and I set in motion and raise the children, continuing his/our legacy.

Single

I am a single female. A widow with two children. Baggage. I didn't have formal "baggage" when Sean and I met. Some like to reframe it: experience. Today's dating scene is completely foreign, not that I was good at the scene in my day, but I feel like the online dating of today is beyond my scope. I viewed my single-dom a bit differently than most anyway. I enjoyed getting to know people and what they were all about and what inspired them and what I could I learn from them. I feel that way about everyone, so I don't know that I am going to be able to change my feathers on this one.

Other People's Issues

Standing alone in a crowd, making every attempt to look and feel like I belong where I am is ever so lonely. Sometimes, I set a challenge, I will take myself out to lunch all by myself. I will take myself to a movie, dancing, hiking anything we used to do together. I challenge myself to be present and stand on my own two feet, even if it is uncomfortable because that is where I belong. It would have been natural as a couple. It is just me, standing balanced on my own two feet now.

I am now a third wheel. Why would I suddenly be ousted from my circle of friends because my husband passed? My friends are my friends. That is that. Or so I thought. On a rare occasion, what I have observed however is something completely different. I have been in social circles with friends and newcomers or insecure females would see me as a threat. What?! Just because I am doing something with a friend of mine, and my friend happens to be male, means just that, my friend and I are out doing something. I had not anticipated needing a shirt that states, "My husband got cancer and died. That does not make me a home-wrecker." I have friends who happen to be guys. I have been coached that is other people's issues, I still don't like it.

I had to re-evaluate where people fit on my Relationship Spiral. My identity changed in some of my "friends" eyes and I am no longer welcome in their social circle because I am single. That was a disappointing surprise to me. As a friend, I let them know I will be there for them if they need a friend, and that although I am no longer married, I as a person, haven't changed.

What has changed is that I have seen life in fast forward and life is short. It is imperative that if I want to accomplish things and create a legacy before my time is through, I need to focus my attention on that and be distracted by things I consider fun and diversion that replenish me to refocus again. I thought about how I accomplished things successfully in the past. I kept my eye on the big picture goal and focused on the details to meet the stepping stones all along the way. I have learned I can get much further, faster in a more streamlined way with fewer mistakes and energy lost when I engage and follow the advice of my teachers, Subject Matter Experts, wise ones, and mentors, all whose guidance prevents costly/timely mistakes and helps me overcome challenges.

Rings

There have been many things I have had to let go of and grieve over once when my late husband passed. A significant issue was how to address a visible symbol of our union, my wedding ring. Did this ring represent our commitment to each other?

What do I do with my late husband's wedding ring? Death did us part, does that mean the contract is null and void? I still felt married. I had to consider my options. The weight of the decision was a heavy one. The answer is to do what brings you comfort. I was comfortable with having the ring on and my late husband alive and well with his ring on. That was super safe. That is no longer an option. The reality of my late husband's absence left me with yet another difficult choice. The ring on my hand told a story that was not in line with my current reality.

I realize in a time when there is little in your control, it is important to be able to make some decisions. This is one of them. It is a personal decision when and what to do with wedding rings.

Leave the ring with him? It holds our vows and represents our relationship, together.

Should I put both rings together on my left hand?

Put it on my right hand?

Put his or both of our rings on a chain?

Take them off and keep them somewhere safe until ready to make a decision at another, less emotional time.

Melt them down and turn them into a new piece of jewelry.

Keep them for the children.

Sell one or both of them and do something valuable with the revenue that makes a positive impact on your future life.

No one recommends throw them in the ocean. However, I know a kid who posted an ad in the local paper after finding a wedding ring in the ocean. No one answered his ad so he has his own plans for that ring.

A dear friend of mine compared my situation to a widow she knows and loves who never moved on from the loss of her husband. This widow talks about her late husband like he is still present in her life and she never moved to another relationship.

My dear friend wants romantic love to come forward into my life. She felt strongly enough to recommend I not follow suit by keeping the physical and social reminders of my being married present in daily life and conversation. Her recommendation is to take off the ring.

I took her advice, a deep breath, and removed the ring. The message I was sending to the world said, "I am married." That is no longer my reality. I slipped the ring off my finger onto a chain holding his ring that remains near where I sleep. My finger was cold, naked, sensitive, empty and alone. Unconsciously, I searched for the ring for months. Similarly, I searched for my missing love. I longed to return the ring to my hand with the hope that my late husband, too, would return. I realize that was not an option. So many things are no longer an option.

Pitfalls: People to Look out for

Subscription Friends

There are social situations that require your presence to be part of the group. The only way to stay in this proverbial school of fish is to be present at each event or have an insider who will tell you where to show up next. Plans for the next social gathering are determined at the current one. If you are not present you are dropped from the subscription and the group. Out of sight out of mind.

Powerful or Popular Friends

You don't really need a lot of friends. Sometimes one or two very close friends are easier to track and more reliable, valuable than a huge social circle that can sometimes be difficult to manage with all the emotions and needs of each of the individuals. There are some who say being popular is being liked by many. Beware the popular people who are actually hidden power mongers and those around them are really just afraid of becoming their next target and that is how they appear "liked" by many. I'd like to say that doesn't last, in fact, these people are well-rehearsed and can create this social leverage in just about any social situation.

Social Status Friends

I'd like to consider these people more network connectors and there are plenty who will actually leverage their position in your best interest. Realize there are also those who step on others to raise their position in society. It is easy to fall prey to people who raise their status by using your inside information and connections. In these circles, be polite and friendly, keep it light, and get them talking about themselves. They will love you for it. The three-corner compliment is another great deflector.

Techniques to Survive Social Situations

How to Make a Friend

Making a friend is easy. Keeping a friend is easy. It is going deep into a trusting, reliable friendship that requires navigation. To make a friend, look someone in the eye and be brave enough to say, "Hi." If you are really going for it, share your name. I actually prefer the way dogs make friends. Based on their life experience, because even dogs may have insecurities and baggage, they approach one another, check each other out and if all goes well, they start to play. Oh, it seems so easy. Why, then, is it so hard? Because you are worried about rejection and if they are judging you and wondering if you fit in the group while allowing your unique qualities to stand out. With all due respect, sometimes I'd prefer to just take one whiff of people and decide whether we should play or not.

What's a Nice Girl like You Doing in a Place like This?

Making first contact

You can initiate a connection in the wild using this technique as a starting point. These days the wild means anywhere in real life, versus the internet.

1. Make eye contact and smile, mirror neurons will copy what you show so do your best to smile cheerfully rather than with anxiety.
   - Attraction is literally two bodies moving closer together. Close the gap between you. Say something. You could start with the simpler version I noted above by initiating a conversation with, "Hi." A more advanced version might be to engage in small talk or ask for help with

something you can't easily find on your phone. People like to feel wanted, needed, and purposeful.

2. Expect this person to be in a committed relationship then the result is you're correct or you have found someone who is available.
   - Hi! What brings you here? You seem like a nice guy; Did you come with your wife or girlfriend? Tell me a little about yourself. What's your story?

3. End on a high note
   - Make a suggestion: I should get going. Give me a call so we can continue this conversation.

4. State your Expectations
   - "Ben" it's been great chatting with you. If you give me a call before the end of the week…. You can call me to set something up for next week.

Keep it fun and light-hearted. When it is your turn to tell your story, keep it high level and turn the conversation back to the moment and the opportunity to build a relationship between the two of you present.

1. Unfortunately, I lost my husband, the children's father a couple of years ago. We had a great life together and now I'm looking forward to meeting someone new.

2. I appreciate your compassion. Let's have fun and keep it positive tonight. I'm happy to share more with you another time.

If it has been a while you could try: As a sole parent, I have a lot of responsibilities raising two kids. I haven't made enough time for myself in the past. But, I'm ready for that now.

Simple right? You got this.

Three-Corner Compliment

The three-corner compliment is a wonderful way to build an ally, and make someone else feel good. Here is how it goes. You are in a group of more than two. You come up with something, anything to say nice about person number two, but the way you bring it up is to get buy-in from person number three. For example, "Hey Lisa, don't you think Amy's hair looks great?" You've allied with Lisa and made Amy feel like a fitting part of the group, who happens to look great.

Three-Point Thank you

1. Thank you for X.
2. X is significant because
3. Thank you again,
4. Note how X will benefit you and how they were thoughtful about gifting you X.

Four-Step Apology

To acknowledge a wrongdoing, we go through a four-step apology in our family.

1. Acknowledge the wrongdoing by stating the part you played in the wrongdoing.
2. Apologize. Come right out and say, "I am sorry."
3. Make it right. Is there a way to correct the situation? If so, offer it up.
4. Commit. It really helps to know what will be implemented to prevent the wrongdoing from happening again.

For example, I should not have laughed when I spilled ketchup all over you. I am sorry for spilling the ketchup and for laughing. Please allow me to help clean up the mess. I wouldn't want you to do that to me. I will make every effort not to spill on you again and I promise not to laugh at your expense.

Do Not Confuse Longing for Connection with Love

Longing for lost affection is real. No one will deny that. As you feel you need connection, find appropriate ways to fill that need.

You know love. Love is a bi-product of connection. Connection in the wrong situation is not a way to fill the need for love.

Romance

I have a bounty of friends at different points on my Relationship Spiral of friendship. Some are in the super-Inner Circle of Trust. I am fortunate to have the capacity for plenty of Inner Circle people, with room for more. None, not one of them are brazen enough to put a legally and emotionally available man in front of me. Not one. I could not expect them to. How could they? I realize there is no replacing my late husband. It will be challenging for my people to accept I might have affection for anyone else. With my late husband gone, I have plenty of affection with no outlets. People look to me when they are looking for him. I understand and try to fill a void, that I cannot. It leaves them wanting and although I am not alone, I am not in a romantic partnership.

The first step in the process is the same as all the others we've been going through: figure out where you stand first. Evaluate where you would like to be going, and within your value system start taking action in that direction.

If I deserve "better," then how come I can't even get attention from the likes of that guy!?

Show up to meet your tribe. Here is the uncomfortable reality of the situation. Your social circles as a widowed woman may need to be adjusted. You may need to expand your current social circle. That can be either challenging, exciting, or both. There are opportunities everywhere and on the rare occasion you will have a guide who welcomes you and introduces you to "the gang." Really it is a matter of finding people you feel comfortable with, who you find entertaining, inspiring, who you share common interests with. That is where to start. What are some of your interests regardless of how vague or unknowledgeable you are on the subject today? What might hold the slightest fascination for you? Cooking, driving, cars, dancing, religion, volunteering, the arts, writing, anything. Here is an opportunity to try something that hadn't happened for whatever reason in your life: take a class, join a choir, engage in the children's school in some capacity. There are so many times in life between events when you shared a moment sitting next to your husband and now it is simply uncomfortable because you are sitting or standing on your own. You are not alone. Stick it out. You may be waiting for the children's school presentation to begin, the Halloween parade, their sporting events. Especially at a time like this, it feels our society is designed for couples, while you are standing there without your significant other.

Once you have positioned yourself in a place where you have an opportunity to connect with others, but they haven't shown up, stay present and stay. It all takes time. When my children are bored, I suggest they look at the big picture. Then pay attention to the details. Take a moment to see the world around you. Notice the environment you are in, the temperature, the smell, the colors, the sounds. Pay attention to the detail in the space, the light juxtaposed against shadows, the textures and minutia provide valuable input to where you are at in the world. Use all your senses. Then move inward and feel your breath stroke the back of your throat, what temperature is the air? How are you placed physically in space? Are you balanced on both legs? Are you stressed anywhere in your body? Can you adjust to release physical tension? Get out there and be available for your tribe to show up eventually.

Recently we went on a cruise. The children and I planned it out to engage in as many conversations as possible so we could meet people straight away. We were tired and just wanted to go to bed. The children did. I wanted to stick to my plan. I called guest services asking if there were singles events. They suggested pickleball and something else equally ridiculous. I read the schedule which included a 9:30 p.m. unhosted singles meetup. Okay, a meetup. That sounds both painful and promising. I dressed. I showed up. I wasn't interested in drinking alcohol so I ordered a Nojoito which was essentially club soda and mint. It looked the part. I was unsure if I looked the part. I attempted to banter with the bartender, the couple nearby and two fellows thirty years my senior. Eventually, there were a few other people who showed up solo. We introduced ourselves to one another. There were no obvious matches in the group. There were no subtle matches in the group. I could see we will need to stick together as the single, unmatched people on the cruise. Unless someone perfect was simply too tired to come out that evening … always hopeful. I went to the disco alone. I set a challenge to sit there for two hours. Just sit and listen to the music and look at the lights, no matter what. Show up in an attempt to find my tribe. There were a few scattered groups at the disco. I got a glass of water and sat. I sat and I sat. The music was not that good. There were a couple of women who knew all the lyrics to any song played. I stayed. Brutal. I could so easily have slipped into bed and gone to sleep. I was going to show up on night one. Eventually, some couple got up to dance and the woman was friendly enough to encourage the others on the dance floor. It did take over an hour, but I got up and danced by myself and the other ladies and I danced together. It reminded me of when we were children and we would turn on the music and dance in the living room. That was enough entertainment. This is how the "Core Four" got its start. That is how I transitioned a lonely vacation to one filled with friendly faces and laughter. And still each friendship has to start somewhere and it is rarely obvious at first blush how important a friendship could be … even if it is only for the duration of a vacation. The feeling of being part of a group is so valuable, it was worth the showing up, even if that part is hard – every time.

Imperfections Required

You are not destined to be only a member in the choir, one voice amongst the others. There will be a time when you will need to take a deep breath and know that others will need your voice to follow – pitchy or on target. Trust yourself.

What do you do with the emotion of feeling embarrassed? What if people laugh at you? Would you laugh at others? Are you so critical of others? Are you so critical of yourself that you would not allow yourself to laugh at yourself and to invite others to laugh at/with you? Welcoming others to see your vulnerabilities and your weaknesses will make you stronger. They are seeing their own susceptibilities when they see yours and when they see themselves in you; it makes them stronger. They will admire you … even if you do not think you are "perfect," because you are perfect just as you are, at each moment in time.

Imperfections make you human. I recently met the man who created synthesized music. He used FM radio waves. People did not want computers to replace real people playing instruments. He wanted computers to enhance what people can do with music. He sold the patent to Yamaha. The royalties are still paying for the

Stanford music department. He wanted to add synthetic voices to his music. However, no one believed the tones as a human voice until he layered the sounds on top of each other and allowed them to waver. Without the imperfection, the sound is not believable as a human voice because these flaws describe our uniqueness. This is an example of how "perfection" is not perfect.

For a while, I expected people to cut me some slack, be nice to me and make things a bit easier because I had lost my husband. I had a major life-role change. Shouldn't everyone understand? Jennifer felt this, too. Initially, I couldn't pronounce the word widow. Then everyone needed to know so I started sharing that information freely. Then prospective dates needed to know it first thing, which backfired completely. Whereas I thought they would like to know I knew how to be in a loving relationship, they would prefer I had been divorced rather than widowed and that was the end of that.

Now I know how to hold my head high, provide the high-level story, and move on to fun and diversion.

CHAPTER 10:

Be Illuminous! – Fun and Recreation

Living fully means accepting all aspects of life, including suffering, anger, pain, and joy. Make trade-offs to ensure your actions match your values. If you were advising someone you care about, you would recommend having fun and enjoying life along the way. There is a heavy cloud that grays life out after loss. Life is more fun in color with good times and laughter. You may feel as if you need authorization to be happy again, but there is no one with the authority to give it except yourself. There is no authorization needed to appreciate the little things in life. Fun and diversion is an exceptional way to find art in living. It may seem like a luxury at first, but neuroscience of mindfulness, gratitude, and happiness suggests the chemical response to laughter and joy is good for you physically, mentally, and spiritually. I have a philosophy that each of us has a figurative gold thread through our bodies. When we are run down, not feeling confident or competent, that gold thread gets thin and brittle. When we are feeling vibrant, this thread enhances and its luminosity flows through and exudes from within, giving us a radiant glow of happiness.

A widow friend of mine, Mary, was surprised that fun and recreation was an area where she needed to expand outside her comfort zone. She realized that she could find something entertaining in the direst of situations, but "in the direst of situations" is not where she wished to spend most of her time. Living is more than just being alive. Mary decided to adjust her approach, take a deep breath, and focus on the good things in the present moment to "come alive" and appreciate the humor and joy in life. She set up some rewards to recognize herself when she achieves some of her goals, as well. She rewarded herself for small accomplishments with walks and talks with friends, manicures, and pedicures, special time with the children, like going to a movie. She set bigger victory recognitions as a gym membership, a new outfit, and a night out with friends.

Accept the Things You Cannot Change and Have Fun Anyway

I've never been the thin one in the room, but I've often been one of the lightest … not in weight but in spirit. As a result, nothing has stopped me from dancing or even teaching physical fitness. I may not be the fastest, the prettiest, the most graceful but I am doing it and I am enjoying what I am doing. My way. This is me. And my story includes my version of fun and diversion. So does yours. I figured it out … and now I will share it with you. The answers are within you, already written and you know them, you just need to allow them to come up.

How do you invite fun and diversion into your life? Ask yourself what has become profoundly important to you over the past year.

Those highlights should point you in the right direction of valuable ways to expend your energy. Here is my list:

There are three things that stand out as profoundly important so I create opportunities for them to be highlighted for myself and my children:

1. Being a strong provider for my family, physically, emotionally, financially and spiritually has always been important to me. These things that I take for granted have come into question. I have to make an effort to ensure they are all in place.

2. Making moments and positive memories. I never lived to make memories, I used to just live. Now I stage activities to "make a memory." I don't know if it is as honest, but we are doing more things as a family together, like playing board games, going to breakfast, and taking a canoe out on the water, taking walks, cleaning the house, whatever it is, we make it a family event.

3. Building and maintaining real relationships with people. Connecting with people, family, and friends are of tantamount value to me. Doing stuff together rather than acquiring stuff.

One Day, Just Start

It took Elizabeth a full year before she went from functionally catatonic to her feeling as if she could reach out and live her life again after her husband passed. Her life orbited her husband and children. She had relied on him for most every aspect of her life, from emotional/financial support, relationships, co-parenting and diversion. Once he had passed, she had been going through the motions, living life for her children by getting them to where they needed to be and that was about all she could do. One day, she woke up and started making plans. Plans to connect socially, plans to take care of herself and her health, plans to re-stabilize and find purpose in her own life as well as the children's routine. She joined religious and community social clubs. She volunteered to do philanthropy in her community. She got involved with the children's friends' families and this is how she rebuilt her Circle of Trust on her Relationship Spiral.

Teamwork, Sustainability, Compassion

In our case, we had adventuring at the top of our list. Adventuring is not for everyone. It is for us. It got us out of the house. Or, we adventured something new in the house. Or, we went to the backyard. Eventually, we adventured the neighborhood and expanded our circle.

You know I am sad. I miss my guy. At the same moment, my heart rips from my chest missing him, I realize how fortunate I am to have had him and his voice in my head reassures me, holds me, and misses me, too. So, it's kind of a pull between heart-breaking and loving-stabilizing. Then the children remind me to be strong and move forward. We decided to Teamwork, Sustainability, Compassion adventure. We did a live-aboard, learn-to-sail program to re-establish teamwork as our new three-person team. And the children wanted to see the places Sean and I visited in Belize, so I emailed my friends in Belize who set us up on a return. We learned about wind, solar and water power, how to sustain a one-mile island. The children and I were in the same room where Sean wrote loving letters to the children for the time after he was gone. Again, mixed emotions everywhere. But we are creating new memories... and most importantly the children and I are a team together.

All along the way, we shared compassion for others. It helped us feel stronger when we realize we had something to share that benefitted others. We helped out at the horse stables. We customized gifts and helped others advance their own ideas and goals on our travels as in Belize where we brought school supplies and clothes. Adventures have given us the opportunity to see how other people live and address life challenges. We brought supplies to schools and medical references to a pediatric hospital in Cuba. Another adventure took us to orphanages in Mexico where we helped prepare meals and shared inspirational craft ideas with the children. We hope these interactions act as catalysts for continued creation and innovation that is appropriate to those people who benefitted from our gifts. So many people helped us with their gifts, to bring us to this day. It feels good to be in a position to remember we have something of value to share as well.

Tips to Enjoy Life's Celebrations and Milestones without Your Spouse

There are several ways to go when facing landmark days without your spouse. You can maintain the traditions and honor him along the way. You can adjust the tradition to the new format of your family. You can create new traditions. Or, you can find some combination of the above. The thing is there are triggers hidden all over the place on these days. What is a girl to do?

In addition to all the other life celebrations throughout the year, Valentine's Day, my birthday, his birthday, our wedding anniversary, his passing day or funeral date would just be another lovely day until the external, social pressure of this anniversary is highlighted. Others lovingly reach out to tell me how much they miss him. I am grateful he made such a positive impact on so many people's lives. How do I get through these days? I appreciate these loved ones for honoring him and keeping him in their hearts and for using those reminders as a touchstone to connect.

Traditions

We would like to stick with traditions. We are starting new traditions. We are bowing out this year. They may be disappointed in you; This is the moment in which they are experiencing a loss because their expectations and traditions have changed. Forgive them and show compassion. Do what is right for you at this time. This is you taking control of your life and what happens in it. (The service levels have decreased.)

Plan Ahead for the Pitfalls

Think of the potential pitfalls. If you were planning a trip somewhere, you would plan the logistics of travel, packing and what to do once you've arrived at your destination. Each portion of the planning, you think through variables that might affect the outcome of the trip. What time should you wake up to catch the transportation? What will you eat when you arrive? Are they open? Have you packed for weather changes and are you prepared to dress appropriately? Then if you are really organized you would record the event and scrapbook the adventure for memory.

You know the challenge days and life celebrations are coming. What can you prepare to make them meaningful and positive for yourself? Invite a friend. Do something special for yourself. Make it so you do not feel like you are missing out.

How to support and comfort others while you are moving through your own grief and figuring out what happens next.

Plan ahead for pitfalls the children may encounter, as well. How can you prepare them for visits with people who may trigger grief for the children? In advance, we plan a few questions to ask visitors. I realize the secret will be out when I share this, but sometimes we play a game, challenging each other to get the conversation going, by competing to get someone else in the group to say a word or phrase that is out of context. The winner is the one who convinced someone at the party to sing any phrase from the National Anthem or something like that.

I dropped the children off at a weekend grief camp that was too far away to drive back and forth, so I got a hotel room nearby … and maybe they would get there and say they couldn't possibly live without me for two nights. Looking back, I think I was planning on sabotaging the whole event so I didn't have to be apart from them. It didn't work. They were fine. What had I done? I sequestered myself all alone in some cheap, old hotel room with a book. I took a walk. I went to a lonely, lousy dinner. Finally, I called for back-up. I reached out to one of my trust circle emotional support friends who showed up for me, with a bottle of champagne and instantly transformed my grief-stricken self-pity party into a girlfriend slumber extravaganza!

Traditional End-of-Year Blues

There are so many things that are different without your late husband. There are some things that are the same as before, but they are escalated because you are head of household and sole parent. It is helpful to differentiate the two. About 75 percent of the way through just about any project is probably the most exhausting point. Energy and enthusiasm are drained and finishing is just about continuing forward. That is no different getting through the year. Preparing the holiday season, whichever that might be for you, can be exhausting. Planning for pitfalls for Thanksgiving is totally plausible, but by the time you've given in to all the sweets and family responsibilities, your willpower has given out. With all the moments of truth that end up in triggered grief, indulgences and pity parties, by the time Christmas comes around everyone feels exhausted and weak. This is no different than in the years before your husband passed. But it is harder without him because he is not there to re-inspire you. Just like the children still need to brush their teeth and clean their rooms even though their dad died, you will need to get things done, too.

Traditions build strong family relations between generations while offering an opportunity for stories and rituals to be shared. They provide a sense of belonging. Inevitably this creates a melancholy situation when your lost loved one is not part of the experience. You could go with it and maintain the routine so the children know what to expect. You could also adjust so it is clear you are honoring those who have passed while living in the present. Another option is to create your own experiences and traditions, not to avoid the past, but to honor the future you are developing. During some of the big holidays, we have created new traditions. On life event days, I challenge myself to do the "positive opposite" by pushing myself just outside my comfort zone to expand my reach as a person.

How do you address traditions? Would you like to stick with them, start new ones? Bow out for a season or two? Others may be disappointed because their expectations and traditions will be changed further by not having you involved. Forgive them and show compassion. Do what is right for you at this time. This is you taking control of your life and what happens in it. (The service levels have decreased.)

Add Another Person to Your Advisory Board – The Fun Meister

When you are ready … and you will know because the information you are taking in will be more about external things than internal emotions and how to address this and that and how do I get up and move on. Your mind will start to nest with other things such as, "How do I pull myself together?" and "What's next?" and "Will I ever really smile and laugh again?" Most importantly you will be asking yourself what action to take to make it all happen and you'll be ready to move on those steps.

Much like developmental stages we and the children went through as we were learning to eat solid food, crawl, toddle, walk, parallel play, engage with others and so on through puberty and engaging with others in personal and professional ways building our own community, there will be a time in this widowhood phase when it is time to make some changes, including letting loose and reclaiming hobbies, past-times, adventures, passions of your own.

This is a phenomenally good time to find and or call upon another mentor/guide for your Advisory Board. This is the person that no matter what when you hang out with them, you laugh. You could be stuck in an elevator and this one would have you laughing until you were set free and then everyone would want to do it, with stories to tell. (I don't actually recommend this. It is a proverbial scenario.) That's the person/group who will help elevate your emotion and infuse effervescence transforming everyday routines into memorable life moments.

Let the Children Play

It may not be believable, but whatever the children are going through at this moment may not last forever. Each age and stage of childhood has its beautiful moments that we as parents are given the life gift of enjoying and experiencing life again through their eyes. We also receive the gift of them knowing that no matter how they treat us, we will unconditionally love them. Those challenging moments are their way of expressing their frustration with the world, their inability to communicate how they are feeling or leveraging their position in the world to attain their goals. (We are no different, I know. Some things never change.) The difference is we have lost our unconditionally loving partner who we used to pillow talk and laugh or eyeball roll about the way the children are behaving and there is almost no one appropriate to share some of these incredible moments with.

Whether it is the life gift of firsts: first rollover, word, solid food, crawl, walk, tumble, pet interaction, friend, sugar, soda (that burns your tongue if you don't remember the first time you tried it), swim, school experience, play date, slumber party, birds and the bees conversations, kiss, relationship, breakup, graduation. These are big moments in life and they are sandwiched between other learning moments that build confidence and sensory experiences and pushing limits and sibling quibbling. All of them teach us what works and what doesn't work. We sequester the middle school children facing the transition from child to adult at an entirely different middle school where we live. It's an entire school of children trying things to determine whether treating someone one way or another achieves what they are going for or not. We hope they (we) learn from these experiences and treat everyone better as a result.

Currently, I have brooding teenagers. It is absolutely brilliant how much effort they put into actually being miserable, obstinate, and defiant. It is as if the more miserable they are now, the cooler they are now and it somehow ensures a place in the popular category later. Whatever happens, they should not under any circumstances allow a picture of their happy faces to be captured in film, especially near a sibling at risk of losing status as possible future popular.

Popular, I've learned is often simply a need to be powerful and in extreme cases, those who ally with the popular are really just in fear of being the next target. One or two friends is way more manageable in many circumstances and are easier to manage.

Come Out and Play

All in all, we are doing well. How much have we endured? How much can we endure? We thought we passed the limit a long time ago. We are all moving at the speed of healing which is much slower than anyone would like. We have no control over the speed. We fought for my late husband's life for years and now we live with grief as our companion. We want to go out and live!

We have been bonding together as a family under emotionally draining circumstances. Now we are focusing on connecting through energy building activities... harder to come up with than I originally thought. We talked about going on a real adventure. Together we deduced the prescription for our family is "play." Everything has been so serious we forgot how to play.

Ancient philosophers, Plato and Aristotle discussed the role of play in education, but specific play theories were not developed until centuries later. In the early 1900s, Maria Montessori postulated that "play is child's work" as it is sensory learning. In the same era, John Dewey positioned play as preparation for children to become healthy working adults. In 1920, Sigmund Freud saw play as a means of releasing painful memories and feelings. Later in 1972, Bruner proposed one of the main functions of child's play was to rehearse actions to various real-life scenarios in a safe, risk-free environment so that when confronted with a difficult situation, it would not be so stressful.

Jean Piaget's theme was playing is a rehearsal. Piaget was most noted for introducing the stages of child development as a way to adjust one's own views to meet the needs of the outside environment. Lev Vygotsky postulated children use play as a means to grow socially. In play, they encounter others and learn to interact using language and role-play.

More recently, The American Academy of Pediatrics highlighted the importance of play in promoting healthy child development and maintaining strong parent-child bonds. The AAP shows play is essential to development because it contributes to the cognitive, physical, social, and emotional well-being of children and youth. Play also offers an ideal opportunity for parents to engage fully with their children. Play is so important to optimal child development that it has been recognized by the United Nations High Commission for Human Rights as a right of every child.

Why should it be reserved for children? Let's all join the game.

One of my favorite parenting techniques puts the focus on nurturing the parent-child connection. One way to implement this is through play listening, which includes having a caring adult create distinct play periods when the child has the upper hand in the play (s)he has chosen, to build an essential connection with the child.

Parents can look for ways to invite their child to laugh for extended periods of time while exploring the more powerful role in the game. This creates a special time for parents and children to be together in an honored place. If you can allocate even a few minutes, and you can specify that 'this game will last fifteen minutes,' you are creating an example of the kind of cooperation and enthusiasm we expect from them at all the other times. When the play is allowed to be child-driven they are practicing decision-making skills, pursuing their own passions, engaging while moving at their own pace.

Some of my favorite memories are the times the children share their world with me through play.

During play listening, I have found myself in fantasy worlds with magical powers as a Pegasus-sister, a mermaid, horse, shape-shifter, spy, ninja and a mischievous student. The children typically choose the opportunity to experience being my equal or my guide.

Secret spoiler alert for parents only! Reading between the storyline of the game, they often share with me metaphors of what is on their mind and what challenges they may be facing.

We were not the first to think we should lighten up a bit, goof off and laugh together. Games are formalized expressions of play capturing ideas and behaviors of people from different time periods. Dice, tiles, boards, tops, and darts have been found in archeological digs all over the world.

As a family, we found a game at the intersection of nearby, reasonable price and entertaining for all … Lawn Bowling. Unlike bocce ball, the "bowls" are weighted heavier on one side which adds an additional dimension to the game. Naturally, the children were fantastic at it and we all had a good time.

When we play, dopamine is released which induces elation, excitement, and orchestrates nerve net development and alignment all over the brain. So, I share our positive prescription with you... play.

CHAPTER 11:

Finding Enthusiasm for the Long Run

Your current reality has changed and eventually, you will need to change with it. There are obstacles in every path and with guidance or experience you will probably learn how to overcome them. Can you anticipate and plan for obstacles that will come up so you are better prepared for them?

What could go wrong? As you have been forced into an identity change, you are morphing into a new you. There is struggle in the transition. Pitfalls, curveballs, and unexpected obstacles arise that you may never have faced had your late husband not died. But here you are, and most of the time it is something you could not have made up.

Your children may feel they have lost both their parents if you don't take the lead as a sole-parent, listening, and guiding to re-stabilize them, reminding them that you will continue to be their pillar of strength. Who knows how this loss will affect them in the long-run. Children are resilient … but these are developmental times.

If you don't take the responsibility for ensuring your expenses don't go beyond your revenue, you could get stuck in financial difficulties. You may lose your job if you aren't meeting the responsibilities you have committed to accomplishing in exchange for a salary which could cause a domino effect of other challenges to face, including career change.

Fearing the pain of loss again may isolate you. If you don't risk being vulnerable enough to build or maintain valuable relationships you may lose connection with others. The risk is necessary to rebuild your Circle of Trust. Others need you as much as you need them.

If you don't have any diversion or recreation it is easy to lose sight of the value in life. Then you have lost even more than your late husband. If you have no reenergizing downtime, you may not be prepared to live a full and happy life again.

I appreciate that my children acknowledge my taking care of myself puts me in a better position to take care of them in the long-run and keeps me happier. Happy mom helps make for happy children. My children acknowledge and trust me more as they see me addressing each aspect of our lives with intention, to ensure we, as individuals and as a family, are becoming the best versions of ourselves. Together we continue to evaluate where we are at on the confidence assessment noted in chapter one and put energy toward the areas that make the most positive impact. Whether they express it to you or not, your children understand at a deep level that when you are well and happy, so too will they be.

Depleted

What makes life valuable? What are the moments that are so important we strive to live for them? Where are the streams of light that contrast the shadows, adding dimension and giving meaning? How do we hold those positive feelings, breath to breath, so we can get through the challenging times, increasing the value of the highlights that carry us through to the next cherished moment when we can exhale, relax and soak it all in?

And how do we see those beautiful moments when our eyes are blurring our vision with tears?

I have inherited some antiques passed down from my grandparents: a favorite lamp, a teacup, a serving utensil with detail hard to find these days. These items have been soldered to the point that the repair is part of the character of the item. These days if something breaks, we repair it to hide it was ever broken or consider it waste and replace it. The art of Kintsugi uses copper powder or gold leaf to mend broken pieces, communicating a sense of history and care. Kintsugi artists believe when something has suffered damage and has a history, it becomes more beautiful.

Before we were certain we were dealing with great loss, I used the "Sad, Mad, Glad" time one night to ask everyone for a list of their favorite things. I was so sad in my heart I felt I might forget what makes us happy. If I had a list of those things, then I could refer to it and remind myself of happy things.

Recently, I felt as if we are at the down-side of this challenging transition, and my spirits continued to rise up.

I found the list of our favorite things. At a high level, we value family, friends, and pets, sharing adventures, celebrating life events, learning, and experiencing and sharing food together. It makes us happy when we see others happy, even better when we are catalysts to others' happiness. We like sharing time with friends, going fast in the water, in cars, on snow, bikes, horses, waves, and ice. We love to indulge in dark chocolate, good champagne, pickles, mangoes and foods from every culture in the world, on sunny days, at the beach, at the cabin on getaways to natural places. We're happy when everybody feels good and love is infused in all of our favorite things.

A long time ago, my grandma and I were walking along a path. She surprised me when she bent down to a bulb plant, bent it in half, and wrapped it around itself. She explained that the plant had done all the growing it needed this season and it is time to turn its energy in on itself to rejuvenate. She transferred it to make it personal: there is a time when it is appropriate to take time to turn your energy inward, release, relax and focus on you so you do not feel depleted. That will replenish and give you the strength to blossom when the time is appropriate.

Songwriter Leonard Cohen's *Anthem* notes that "There is a crack in everything. That is how the light gets in …" illuminating a vulnerability to highlight it as a bright spot, almost pushing us to feature our uniqueness rather than hiding it and the wounds that may go along with it.

The origin of the Kintsugi practice comes from a story of a wealthy fifteenth century man who was not happy with how his precious broken teacup was repaired until he found a craftsman who used gold resin to make it more valuable and appealing with its history revealed. We could compare how we repair and replenish ourselves, our literal and emotional scars, customizing our own personal history, making us more valuable, meaningful and beautiful.

When it came time to consider refilling our "emotional bucket" with fun and diversion, I drew a blank. I felt the external oppression of the widow can't have fun. The children felt the same way. It took a mindset shift to be able to feel that it was okay to even crack a grin, laughing took forever. I went back to our list of favorite things again and again because I kept forgetting it was okay to be happy and have fun again. Enjoying adventures tops our list. When we were out of our environment others didn't know we were not supposed to be happy … and it freed us up.

The science of happiness suggests that the search for happiness could prevent us from finding it and we should be going for a state of satisfied well-being rather than a constant state of enthusiasm. However, I am still going to call it "happy" rather than "satisfied."

Is Happy Just through That Hoop?

You have the key to your own happiness. There is tremendous responsibility in that. Wouldn't it be easier to simply place responsibility in someone else's hands? Well, that could go any which way. If you choose that path, realize the consequences involved include being satisfied with the choices they make even if they don't provide you with the outcome you wish. I am always amazed but rarely surprised at how often I see people pushing blame for their circumstances on others rather than taking the reins of their lives and doing the work to achieve the reward. And by the way, an earned reward is always more satisfying.

Is happy here or is it just over there through that hoop? Growing up, my fantastic and positive thinking mother, was famous for setting my sights just beyond the next horizon whenever I was bored or sad. "When school starts again, when summer arrives, after your next birthday, when you can drive, when you get a boyfriend, when you go to college, when you graduate college, when you get a job, when you get married, when you have children… gosh the hoops with the promise of wonderment were always set out just beyond where I was at. I appreciate she always set my sights forward rather than allowing me much time to remain stuck in any one phase. I had to figure out on my own how to be happy in the moment rather than hoping for happy to come later.

I wish I could undo this for you, but you don't have that as an option. The only way to go is forward. People have different approaches to life. Some have checklists, accomplishments they must achieve and bucket lists. Others find bliss in being present in the moment and allowing the world to bring what may. Regardless, happiness is a state of being.

Being Unprepared Has Its Disadvantages

Although it is challenging to find a one-size-fits-all how-to-do-life-right guide, you are not the first to go through this life experience thing. Experience and statistics show there are plenty of pitfalls, chutes, that you might be able to plan for, avoid or put a solution in place that compensates for the unexpected.

At some point you will start to wish for more from your life. You will notice your thoughts are not so much in the past, but you may wonder how to move into the future. There is plenty of frustration in this phase because you've allowed plenty of space for yourself to grieve…and all that might have included, loss of health, emotional well-being, revenue, active guidance for the children. One day, you will see that more than "right now" is relevant. It might be as a result of the children needing you to help them prepare for their future. It might be that you set your sights a little further out simply by tipping your head up when you walk to initiate the transition. You will start to focus on more than this moment and you will know it is time to take action and take control of your life.

Finding the right current Advisory Board is key. It is often the biggest challenge to find the right people with the right skills to help you do the right thing. And it is not uncommon to rely on people or crumble under your need to please others and their expectations of you.

Position your Inspirational Advisory Board to support you and the children emotionally, and build your network. Not having the right relationships around you and their emotional support makes it challenging to get back into the groove of your life. Surrounding yourself with energy suckers who force you into the grooves that don't serve you is demeaning and detrimental to your stress levels and health as well as the children. You may make mistakes if you don't access experts to coach you with some of your challenges. As much as an Attorney will help detail directives, you can access direction along your path now. As well, not having accountability and network partners puts you in a position in which you don't have people who will help you ensure you meet your landmarks and introduce you to the people and opportunities to get you where you need to go next.

Stress Causes Health Changes

Losing your husband is a tremendous loss. You may feel broken. With the loss of a parenting partner, the secondary losses that follow include loss of general security, health, identity, income, dreams for the future, best friend and confidante, faith, social status, confidence, home, intimacy, job, financial security, support system, working memory, energy, income, and all because a primary person in your life died.

On the Holmes and Rahe Stress Scale, the greatest stressor is the death of a spouse or parent, followed by divorce, marital separation, and imprisonment. As the death of a spouse is often followed by other life changes the stressor factor increases which puts widows and their children at great risk of health concerns.

Preventing Risky and Dangerous Behaviors

Secure your own health and put things in place to care for the general health of the children. Or you may not be strong enough to sole parent your children and where will that leave them? Or they may get lost in a depression or dangerous behaviors that could cause the entire family potentially life-threatening stress, illness or further loss. If you don't stabilize your general health and select some things that will catapult you in the direction of your ultimate goals, how will you change where you are at now? If you are content with how things are now, that is not an issue. Remember to consider how long you have resources to cover your current situation, to determine if not changing your life is the right choice. You know life is short and you have a legacy to create and children to guide so implement self-care to move yourself in that direction.

A recently met a woman who wished she hired me for her sister when her brother-in-law died. Her sister was stuck in grief and could neither help her children or position surrogates to help. The children got involved in risky and dangerous behaviors. One took his life, leaving further disaster and tragedy. The other disengaged completely. The sister remains depressed and is a ward of her family who wishes they hired me as The Widow Guide.

Shedding the Masks on the Family Tree

If continuing a relationship with your late husband's family serves you it is important to make an effort to maintain that relationship. It is key for the children to have extended relatives (related by blood, family tree or love) to know they are part of something bigger than they are. Sofia realized she married the whole family when she married her husband. They have experienced a great loss, as well. It may be even more important for them to remain connected. Those are all individual choices that rely on the circumstances.

How to Prepare for New Intimacy

Some feel strongly that you fall in love once and marry once, like geese. If your man is gone, you are done with that aspect of your life. That is their opinion. You may have found and lost a soul mate. You can have more than one soul mate.

Some feel you should be in a relationship again.

Some say, "You wouldn't consider getting married again, would you?" as if you had committed some terrible crime considering finding another partner. With these types of comments, the voice in my head repeats, "Find the point of compassion. She appreciates her loyalty to her husband and provider. I no longer have a husband and provider. She can't possibly understand. Nor do I wish her to have this insight. I am happy for her. I'm certain she meant well."

"It's too soon." Or, "Why have you waited so long?"

Let it go. Everyone's opinion is impossible to appease.

You follow your own path.

How will your family and community deal with you considering a new partner? At what point will they support you, or free you up for that? That is a conversation you do not need to rush into. Those are choices you make for yourself. It is not for others to decide what is right for you and your children. It is okay for you to move on and have/be a partner again without their authorization. If you need it; I give it to you now. Other people have opinions on the matter. If you listened to other people's opinions all the time who knows how you would have turned out … pretty bland, very acceptable. Following your own heart and desires is the only way to go.

When I was trying to please everyone, remember the advice, "Where are your Wonder Woman cuffs and shield?" Let other people's ideas of how you behave be their own. This is another reminder not to superimpose other people's judgments into your own self-talk.

Sharks and Minnows

Modern psychology suggests children should have small disappointments. But the issues you are facing are real and big. There seems to be no end of tears. I listen to my children cry as if I were someone outside, listening in. I had nothing left with which to comfort them. The desperate weeping sounds, helpless, futile, lost in forced surrender, hopeless. There was a wailing I didn't know could come from them. I cannot care who observes because their screams are for someone who can no longer hear them. My heart breaks. One day I heard the sound of my children's cry change. And then my daughter stops. Full stop. She flatly declared, "Crying is just crying. It doesn't help."

What is right for you is right for your children. Similarly, guide them to follow their own path. As a parent of children who do not fit the norm, this is a constant struggle partly because everyone wants what is best for them ... which is the normal expectation. We try and try and try but you can't put a square peg in a round hole. You know that is why manhole covers are round? So they don't fall in and they fit no matter which direction you drop them on the hole. My children don't fit there.

Exposing the children to all types of activities so they can have an understanding of many things and then they can choose their own passions is the goal. When he was very young, we signed Kevin up for soccer ... for the third time. We were convinced it is a great sport he should enjoy the camaraderie, the running, the game. This time it was in the middle of the weekend. The fireballs were dressed in their adorable red, black and white uniforms. We spread out the picnic lunch because this was the big event smack dab in the middle of the weekend. The coaches set up the game of sharks and minnows. The idea was the coaches were the sharks and the children were the minnows who were supposed to kick the ball across the field to the other side with the coaches attempting to make it difficult for them. Ready, steady, go! That is when it happened. Kevin threw his arms out preventing his beloved teammates from moving forward.

Stop! Don't go there! There are sharks.

The children froze.

No one took a step.

Why would they enter the shark-infested field? The coaches looked at us. We looked back at them. They expected us to change our son. I suggested they change the game to a more positive experience like getting the magic gem across the troll field to the castle to save the fairies from extinction or something. We were at a standstill, literally. Was Kevin wrong? No. Were the coaches? No. There was certainly a disconnect. Our creative kid wasn't going to make it in soccer unless there was a more motivating plot. He is much more interested in computers and 3D modeling original designs than team sports to this day. Finding the right outlet for the children to pursue their passion is a true gift.

Nourish, Balance, Inspire

Nourish

You do everything you possibly can to make everyone as content as possible. How do you refuel your energy so you don't feel physically, emotionally, mentally, spiritually, and financially exhausted? How do you nourish yourself? Really nourish yourself? You could start by putting yourself first once in a while. If you establish boundaries people will stop taking advantage of you and respect your boundaries. You do have to set them up first, though. If you delegate age-appropriate tasks to the children, you are giving them something they can control and feel proud of accomplishing as well as setting the model for them. All this while you are possibly creating space for a little self-care. Here are things you can do to nourish, balance and inspire yourself:

- Put yourself first
- Eat food that nourishes and literally feeds your body
- Realize your vision
- Find Inspiration
- Fulfill your senses
- Engage in things that fill your heart with love
- Participate in happy relationships
- Actively experience emotions
- Pursue intellectual curiousness

Balance

- De/compartmentalize
- Pause
- Breathe
- Find inner joy
- Care for self first
- Speak to yourself as you do with loved ones

Consider using the positive opposite in the moment. Purposely take a breath and use a calm voice rather than yelling when you are angry. It puts you in a more powerful position and in control of your actions. With the children, explain appropriate consequences rather than threatening them, especially with things you would not wish to follow through on. Give them small, immediate consequences instead. Treat them how you would like to be treated. I lost my patience with the children when it took forever to get into the car. My solution? I would sing, "Turn around, sit down, get into your car seat." The children knew the song was coming and would sit down and buckle up to avoid the tune. Hah!

Inspire

How do you find inspiration? Try a desirable approach by playing or seeing the folly in the world around you. Pursue intellectual curiosity and innovation. Reframe a situation by seeing the positive in it. That is a way to stick with someone through the hard times and make the best of them. It is inspiring to receive the gift of help and at some point, you'll be able to do the same for others.

Grit and Sisu

It is depressing to realize just how much we've slipped in our efforts to build our strength. I feel depleted from using whatever willpower and creative solutions I could generate to step up and stand up for the strength of my family and myself.

They say, "Care for the caretaker." The caregiver gives everything, and then some. A word was generated for the ability to withstand life's challenges: grit. Another word is coming into the popular vernacular: sisu. It represents the ability to keep going despite all depleted resources.

Grit and sisu sound like story characters that get through just about everything together. Spiritually we've gone further and deeper than we thought possible. You'll learn community will help if you share your vulnerabilities and ask. Sharing where you are at with your Relationship Spiral will provide you with the grit and sisu to carry on.

Time for the Rebuild

Time heals all wounds, they say. That requires so much more than just patience though. So much is happening below the surface as even a physical wound is healing. If my experience could help you expedite yours, realize some things happen concurrently and other times one thing needs to happen before progressing to the next.

Just as I am walking you through the different steps/aspects that rely on each other to healing grief and finding your way to living your full and happy life as a widow and sole parent, your body uses different systems to heal a physical wound. You can develop a comprehensive healing/rebuilding plan when you know what is involved in each step. According to a study published in the World Journal of Surgery, there are six physical wound healing stages, each of which rely on one another in order to completely close a physical wound:

1. "Rapid hemostasis refers to actually stopping the bleeding through vasoconstriction, like turning off a leaky faucet."
   - In our process, ensure your legal, financial, and emotional systems are in balance.
2. "Inflammation alerts your body to injury and dictates where to send healthy cells but if it goes on for too long, it can actually prevent regeneration."
   - As you stabilize and move through grief, you can focus on where your energy should be allocated rather than getting stuck in a cycle that could spiral you in a negative direction or depression.
3. "All kinds of cells, including those responsible for proliferation and migration are released when inflammation occurs. Cells are called to action in a carefully coordinated process that involves moving in a specific order. Meanwhile, proliferation is similar to hemostasis, as cells work to further constrict your blood vessels."

- Setting a target and actionable items that are in line with your value system sets the scaffolding and trajectory for re-strengthening your life plan.

4. "Angiogenesis occurs when the bleeding is under control. Then, the body begins the process of rebuilding tissue, forming new blood vessels. This process occurs when your body's cells begin to replace the veins and arteries that were damaged, either creating new sections or adding onto existing portions. It's a decidedly complex endeavor, with many chemicals activating to facilitate these new structures."

- This is similar to accepting where you are at now in life and doing the work to become the best next version of you.

5. "Re-epithelialization: Once your body has begun to regrow veins, it's time to begin re-growing damaged skin. Your epidermis is comprised of cells called keratinocytes, and during the re-epithelialization process, your body has to begin forging these chemical components. The process involves the creation of several layers, each working in tandem to offer protection and prevent fluid loss."

- Acknowledge how far you've come and adjust to ensure you are navigating in your best direction. Continue to find ways to enjoy the journey.

6. "Synthesis: Though it's seen as the last step, synthesis often happens almost simultaneously. In this process, certain proteins form blood clots, which helps further prevent bleeding as new skin and veins are formed. There are a number of proteins at play, and certain people lack those necessary proteins to form blood clots."

- You will become the parent and person you wish to be as you re-energize yourself between steps in the right direction.

We evaluate our actions and their consequences in a similar way. For me, there are times to indulge and opportunities to move slightly outside my comfort zone as a means to recuperate and enrich my own life experience. Make a list of positive activities that not only move you in the direction of your ultimate goals, they re-energize you.

CHAPTER 12:

The Beginning of Your New Life Worth Living

These are the steps to move through a difficult time of life. A time no one prepares you for, losing your husband and remaining as a sole parent. You have done so many hard things in your life. You can do this, too.

You Are Not Alone on the Journey

You have done so many things that are hard. You understand the vulnerability and value of being in a marriage and a parent. In this book, you have learned your superpowers and how they serve you, as well as how to neutralize and compensate for weaknesses. You saw how accepting, forgiving and feeling gratitude for where you are now helps you to understand your starting point. You connected with your future self, aligned your target vision to determine your trajectory, as well as acknowledged guides and landmarks along the way. All of this creates a clear path of steps to build and access your support system: your Circle of Trust within your Inspirational Advisory Board on your Relationship Spiral. With your support systems in place, you can move forward with confidence to re-stabilize yourself financially, legally, take control of your health and self-care, as well as be a resourceful and supportive parent. You are in a position to build strong revenue sources, evaluate the alignment of your career, recalibrate your relationships, and know when and how to kick up your heels and have a good time. All this balanced with rest and re-energizing your full and happy life as a widow and sole parent.

Trust yourself! You know you have the answers. Sometimes, they are sequestered deep in the coral reef of your internal self. If you quiet down enough to ask the right question, you know your right answers are deep within.

You know what it is to be in a marriage and a loving relationship. That has not changed. Take what you've learned to make the decisions that need to be made for your family, yourself, your children and continue on experiencing life to the fullest. He may be gone. But all is not gone. We around you will be here to support and guide you along the way. You may falter, but you will not fail. Prioritize and live life fully!

UNVEILING

Dear Sean,

Any days apart were too many, since the moment we met. Once we spent ten days apart. It was too many and we never let that happen again until death do us part. It has now been thousands of days since we've been apart. It is too long and I miss you every day. What have I learned in this time?

Well, once I threatened to leave you because you left your sock drawer open. In fact, I was so upset by it that Rachel and I left you for the weekend. You told me I couldn't live without you. Amongst our weekend adventures, we prayed you would learn to close the drawer.

In this year without you, I learned this was the only thing that bothered me. That was all I could come up with to push against and create struggle for nothing. What a luxury you were.

I have learned that when I mention how much we loved each other, it sounds braggadocios if those other people have not known true love. I wish it for everyone. Good love is good.

I have learned who is my real family … related by blood, related by love, who is brave enough to stand alongside me, even if it is hard. I was surprised to learn who could not stand alongside.

I have learned to find guides for myself and the children who will share their expertise. It is an exhausting challenge to find the right person for the right job and sift through the help that is not helpful.

I've learned that even the most generous of guides can only bring their experience. Thank you for making many years easy, interesting, and fun for me by sharing your vast talents. You were really amazing at so many things.

I learned how much I miss your help parenting the children. They know you are in their hearts, but they also know you are no longer here for kisstribution, "Sad, Mad, Glad," to pick them up from school, to pick out a movie, a computer, a new way of doing new math. You were able to notice things that seem to take me forever to figure out.

I learned how much I miss our specialization and how much courage it requires for me to take on your area of expertise. But I am doing it. Every time.

I learned joy holds every moment of sadness I feel for your loss because of how grateful I am for having had you in my life. I learned your voice in my head is as kind as ever. Your voice in my head would hold me if you could, would help me if you could, and would fix my computer if you could. But, you can't so I accept it … or call someone else. Your voice in my head reminds me to move forward without you.

I learned that people I meet now may never have known you and they missed so much because you would have insightfully made them feel secure and confident and brilliant and interesting and *so* good-looking … and when I tell them about you, they understand they have missed out on you.

I miss you. But I learned I didn't miss out on you. I got you and I feel so fortunate that I was your favorite. I know I was loved in a most wonderful way. And what tremendous gifts you have shared with me.

I learned that I enjoyed all of our adventures together and we were right: ten days were too many to be apart. Sometimes I cry hot, syrupy tears and it is hard to breathe without you. But, I will. I learned that our children are our legacy and they are as amazing and wonderful as we could ever have hoped.

I learned that much of what I know, I learned from you. I have learned that I have the ability to love deeply and there is value to that.

I have chosen to continue to walk this path without you, even if it is hard, strengthened by having had in you in my life. I miss you and love you with all my heart and then some, for always and forever, near and far and close.

ACKNOWLEDGMENTS

Thank you to my late husband Sean who although is now in my past, showed me the value of true love. My gratitude to our children we welcomed into the world, Kevin and Rachel who as well as giving me a reason for living each day and inspire a positive legacy for the future, they keep me entertained and intrigued at every moment.

I extend appreciation to all in our community who held us up, who sent us on adventures to remember to live fully, which provided us opportunity to help others in ways we would not have seen, had we stayed hidden under the bed, hoping the grief monster would disappear.

Thank you to the wonderful Anna Brosler, Teri Roseman, Kirsten Barrington-Hughes, Victoria Lavi, Carolyn Nash, Scott Gordon, Susan Athey, Beth and Guy Kawasaki, Sean and Shalien Riordan, Amanda Goodroe, Cliff and Debbie Young, Meredith Peterson, Leslie Messmer, Julie Grabscheid, Audrey Gold, Steven Ward, Bette Sovinee, Andrea Boje, and Erica Catic…you are all on my Inspirational Advisory Board.

As well, I would like to thank my family related by blood and family related by love, my Circle of Trust, everyone on my Relationship Spiral who helps make me who I am. Thank you for calling on me, knowing so clearly I have value to offer even in my most vulnerable moments.

Everyone has a story. Thank you for being witness to ours. We have learned many things as we have rebuilt our full and happy lives after loss. One of the greatest lessons is how important it is to feel part of something bigger than ourselves.

We are so grateful for the connection and relationships we have built with you and our community because we don't feel so alone. The right words are hard to find.

Thank you. We never imagined being in a situation wherein we needed this level of compassion and support. Thank you for being that for us.

Thank you to Angela Lauria and The Author Incubator's team, as well as to David Hancock and the Morgan James Publishing team for helping me bring this book to print.

THANK YOU

I hope this book and community provides compassion and ease for you.

This book is more than what you hold in your hands. There is so much more I want to share with you to help you get where you would like to be. Due to space constraints, I couldn't fit the entire community you have accessed on these pages. Please join me at TheWidowGuide.com for my list of favorite ways to address some of life's most challenging moments and utilize them as stepping stones in the direction of your goals!

I would love to hear how you are using these tools to support your children and make your Life Worth Living. Go to TheWidowGuide.com and tell me what is going on with you.

"I see you. I hear you. And what you say matters to me." If you are ready to put things in order to become the person you wish to be and strengthen your sole-parenting skills, contact me and learn about the top challenges widows are facing and how they overcame them.

ABOUT THE AUTHOR

Michelle Hoffmann is a Master Coach in Life and Business. She is an author, successful entrepreneur, and dynamic, entertaining motivational speaker. She specializes in helping widows and sole parents re-stabilize their lives after loss to live a full and happy life, though she holds the title of Director of Business Development in a variety of industries.

For over two decades, she has catapulted successful careers working with executives, managers, and corporate employees. She is on the Board of several organizations, including the local Parents Club, Arts Council, a San Francisco school, and she is a Scout Leader. Her local Chamber of Commerce has honored her with Ambassador status.

Michelle is passionate about helping people create a life worth living despite loss. When Michelle's late husband passed away, she adjusted her professional writing and consulting to more personal support. It was at a workshop she delivered to Silicon Valley's Reboot Accel, an organization that helps women rejoin the workplace after a gap in employment, where Beth and Guy Kawasaki inspired Michelle to write a practical and compassionate guide to help widows and sole parents.

She lives in San Francisco with her children and loves running with her Dalmatian, Pixel. Her love for fine company and a good party led her to major in "dinner" at the California Culinary Academy. She balances her culinary appreciation and sense of adventure, by coaching and teaching fitness in North and Central America, Europe, and Australia.